THE POETRY OF
EMILY DICKINSON

CHARLOTTE ALEXANDER
DEPARTMENT OF ENGLISH
NEW YORK UNIVERSITY

D1475939

MONARCH
PRESS

23817

Published by
MONARCH PRESS
a Simon & Schuster division of
Gulf & Western Corporation
Simon & Schuster Building
1230 Avenue of the Americas
New York, N.Y. 10020

Standard Book Number: 0-671-00780-7

Library of Congress Catalog Card Number: 66-1863

MONARCH PRESS and colophon are trademarks of Simon & Schuster, registered in the U.S. Patent and Trademark Office.

Printed in the United States of America

CONTENTS

EMILY DICKINSON

(1830-1886)

EARLY LIFE.   Emily Dickinson was born in Amherst, Massachusetts, in 1830, where she died in 1886. Edward Dickinson, her father, was a lawyer and Treasurer of Amherst College. Given this background, which included an education more extensive than usual for young women of that period—two years at Amherst Academy and one at Mount Holyoke Female Seminary—we can assume that the intellectual and social life of the Amherst College community was available to Emily Dickinson. Schoolgirl recollections of her picture a young woman who was shy but fun-loving, not beautiful but somewhat striking and very neat in dress. For whatever reasons—and modern commentators have been more and more cautious in assigning "reasons," such as the disappointment of unrequited love—she began to lead a rather solitary life about 1853, when she was twenty-three. A letter of that year remarks, "I do not go from home." Her solitude does not seem to have taken a morbid turn, however, until the death of her father in 1874. The fact remains, nevertheless, that from age thirty on, her life was essentially withdrawn from society; and after 1874 she practically never left the family house.

"LOVE AFFAIRS."   About Emily Dickinson's private life a few facts are known, but most of the emotional overtones so indispensable to a full picture must be deduced from her poems and letters. It cannot be said too quickly or too often that her poetry *is* her personality; yet it must be added that in her written expressions we cannot be at all sure of proofs of her emotional life. Indeed, an enigmatic quality, a secretiveness, is one of the essentials of her poetry. There are several men, however, who may be safely mentioned as having influenced her, if we are correct in connecting fact with the inferences in her poetry and letters. During her school years two young men encouraged her

5

interest in books: Leonard Humphrey, principal of Amherst Academy, and Benjamin F. Newton, a law student in her father's office. Newton also displayed an interest in her poetry. It seems likely that these two men, who died young, are referred to in the lines:

> I never lost as much but twice,
> And that was in the sod;
> Twice I have stood a beggar
> Before the door of God!

CHARLES WADSWORTH.   The "love of Emily Dickinson's life," however, is generally assumed to have been a Philadelphia minister with whom she came in contact early in 1854: Charles Wadsworth, 41 years old, married, with a family. Conjectures on young Emily's passion for Wadsworth are based on drafts of three letters to him (although no letters, if there were any, have remained from the Rev. Wadsworth himself) and on the "love poems" which followed in the early 1860's. Wadsworth did call on her in 1860, while visiting in nearby Northampton, and it seems likely that she was aware in 1861 of his intention to move to San Francisco. (Her poems of this period, for example, speak of fears and a sense of loss—"I had a terror since September, I could tell to none. . . .") There is no real evidence, though, for assuming that this unfulfilled love affair was the sole or sufficient motive behind her gradual withdrawal from society; it is more realistic to conclude that such an experience might have encouraged what was already a tendency toward solitariness and introversion in her.

JUDGE OTIS LORD.   Although her last years amounted to a rigid retreat from the world, especially after 1874, letters again indicate—surviving drafts of 15 letters written between 1878 and 1883—that she came to care for Judge Otis P. Lord of Salem, a widower and an old family friend, to the extent that she even considered marriage.

THOMAS WENTWORTH HIGGINSON.   The other name of significance to Emily Dickinson's personal and professional life is that of Thomas Wentworth Higginson, a rising young literary man in 1862 when the young woman sent him some poems to examine. (Higginson was writing for *Atlantic Monthly* at the time.) Their correspondence and an interview survive, although Higginson actually saw her only twice. It can be said, then, that Higginson's essay on her, however meager, is the only one we have from a literary figure of the period. The essay appeared in *Atlantic Monthly* five years after her death. It quoted some of her letters and poems and described his impressions of her. It is a most interesting document in its reproduction of excerpts of Miss Dickinson's letters to Higginson over the years. The correspondence which began with her need for a mentor is pathetically illuminated in the first line of her first letter to him— "Mr. Higginson,—Are you too deeply occupied to say if my verse is alive?" Indications are that Higginson, busy and urbane essayist and academician, whose replies were less frequent than hers, found her poetry quaint, puzzling and of course "insubordinate" with respect to the traditional rules of poetry. To his continuing gentle reproach of "waywardness" in her poetry, Emily replied in the following manner, at once apologetic and unmoved: "You think my gait 'spasmodic.' I am in danger, sir. You think me 'uncontrolled.' I have no tribunal." In another letter she asks Higginson (addressing him usually as "Dear Friend"): "Are these more orderly? I thank you for the truth. I had no monarch in my life, and cannot rule myself; and when I try to organize, my little force explodes and leaves me bare and charred."

A FAMILY MONARCH: EMILY DICKINSON'S FATHER.   It may be that there was a "monarch" in Emily Dickinson's life, though: her stern Calvinist father. Again, this is illuminated in her correspondence, especially in remarks to Higginson, and in what is known of the family relationship. Neither Emily nor her only sister married, and it is generally assumed that Mr. Dickinson dominated the household of mother, two daughters and a son. He did so with less harshness than we might assume, although he stressed Bible-reading over other books which, Emily reports to Higginson, he feared would "joggle the mind." When Higginson visited her, and she told him of much of her early life, "her father was always the chief figure," he records. He was a "man who had from childhood inspired her with such awe, that she never learned to tell time by the clock till she was fifteen, simply because he had tried to explain it to her when she was a little child, and she had been afraid to tell him that she did not understand, and also afraid to ask anyone else lest he should hear of it." There is no need, however, to distort this picture into a warped relationship between father and daughter; it was not the free exchange which we would like to think characterizes the 20th century, yet it certainly was not unnatural for the time. But perhaps Emily Dickinson herself has spoken most accurately of her father, in a letter to Higginson after Mr. Dickinson's death in 1874. It is a touching letter, expressing a tender and awesome regard for the father, and a pathetically "lost" feeling which reaches out to her friend Higginson. It is of course also "poetic," since it contains the same quaintness and elaborate conciseness of her poetry. Instead of stating conventionally, "I would rather have died before he did," she says, "I am glad there is immortality, but would have tested it myself, before entrusting him." To her friend she speaks starkly, out of a terrible loneliness, "I have wished for you, since my father died, and had you an hour unengrossed, it would be almost priceless. Thank you for each kindness. . . ." And of her father she speaks almost in epitaph: "His heart was pure and terrible, and I think no other like it exists."

EMILY DICKINSON'S SECLUSION.   That Emily Dickinson chose to live a secluded life is obvious, but the reasons for this choice are not clear; since her death and the expanding publication of her poems, her editors and biographers have been at pains to point out that neither a love disappointment nor invalidism can be counted as valid causes for her solitariness. Higginson writes, "A recluse by temperament and habit, literally spending years without setting her foot beyond the doorstep, and many more years during which her walks were strictly limited to her father's grounds, she habitually concealed her mind, like her person, from all but a very few friends; and it was with great difficulty that she was persuaded to print, during her lifetime, three or four poems." Her famous seclusion seems to be a matter of "personality," and the keys to that personality lie in such phrases as "habitually concealed her mind" and "a very few friends"; for her poetry and her letters suggest (a) an inveterate secretiveness, and (b) an idealism of human relations probably easily disappointed.

CONCEALMENT OF SELF. Concealment of personal facts and private thoughts is the very framework of her poetry, coupled with a paradoxical desire to reveal the very things she obscures in the telling. These are the descriptive terms most often applied by critics (and the validity of these terms will be evidenced in the analyses which follow): epigrammatic, terse, puzzling. Some of her poems almost appear as riddles as we attempt to decipher from them: "I never lost as much but twice" and:

> My life closed twice before its close;
> It yet remains to see
> If Immortality unveil
> A third event to me. . . .

Whether it is sheer human loss or personal loss Emily Dickinson so frequently recounts, we can never be sure. Her so-called love poems address a "you" with an intensity that cannot help but arouse the reader's curiosity. For example, there is the poem which begins:

> I cannot live with you,
> It would be life,
> And life is over there
> Behind the shelf

> The sexton keeps the key to,
> Putting up
> Our life, his porcelain,
> Like a cup
>
> Discarded of the housewife. . . .

Or to illustrate pure childish efforts of concealment (and both loneliness and mistrust of one's fellows), there is the description of how she reads a letter, the first two stanzas of which read:

> The way I read a letter's this:
> 'Tis first I lock the door,
> And push it with my fingers next,
> For transport it be sure.
>
> And then I go the furthest off
> To counteract a knock;
> Then draw my little letter forth
> And softly pick its lock.

HER IDEALISM.   A second possible reason for her seclusion is that she was an idealist in human relations, expecting too much of people—and of God and religion, for that matter. Her poetry indicates a disenchantment both with present life and with the promise of heaven, doubts which were startling for the period in which she lived. The following poem supports this possibility:

> It dropped so low in my regard
> I heard it hit the ground,
> And go to pieces on the stones
> At bottom of my mind;
>
> Yet blamed the fate that fractured, less
> Than I reviled myself
> For entertaining plated wares
> Upon my silver shelf.

The reference might be to family, a friend, or to the Calvinist religion she had been conditioned to; but it is clear that something or somebody has failed to live up to her expectations. The lines "for entertaining plated wares/ Upon my silver shelf" speak of value which fell below her standards. Or we can turn to that poem well-known among the numerous poems which seem to refer to her seclusion. The first stanza reads:

> The soul selects her own society,
> Then shuts the door;
> On her divine majority
> Obtrude no more.

And the poem closes thus:

> I've known her from an ample nation
> Choose one;
> Then close the valves of her attention
> Like stone.

Is it, then, unrequited love which the poet speaks of here? And if it is, what questions must be posed about the personality of such a poet, whose ideal will permit no substitutes to "obtrude"?

EMILY DICKINSON AND THE CALVINIST RELIGION OF HER DAY. Emily Dickinson's most powerful poetry, as will be seen in the poetic analyses, dwells upon the subject of permanence and decay; or put another way, on time, death, eternity. We must then assume that the religion of her particular background and era exerted a strong influence on her thinking. The result of this religion, however, was to place her in a limbo between faith and doubt. Her father is often referred to as an old-rank Puritan (the terms Puritan and Calvinist are used interchangeably here, and indicate sternness and narrowness), and her family life was undoubtedly filled with typical Calvinist stern observances. Bible reading, prayer meetings, strict keeping of the Sabbath, convictions of eternal damnation or future paradise, suspicions that pleasure was sinful, were the backbone of her father's religion. Yet it is obvious from her poetry that Emily Dickinson developed into a mixture of Puritan and freethinker, and that she was troubled enough by doubts about traditional Calvinist doctrine to treat God and religion from time to time in a poetically flippant fashion. A choice example of such an attitude is also one which illustrates her directness and ironic wit:

> Faith is a fine invention
> For gentlemen who see;
> But microscopes are prudent
> In an emergency!

On the other hand, some of her most beautiful, successful, and often most popular poems are affirmations of faith. We have the following examples (referred to by first lines, which is the customary manner of indexing her untitled poems; these poems will be discussed more fully below): "Because I could not stop for Death"; "I died for beauty"; "As imperceptibly as grief"; "There is a certain slant of light"; and the well-known "I never saw a moor."

LATE QUESTIONS.   Late in her life, however, her questionings about death and immortality became somewhat morbid, as evidenced in the tone her poetry took and in the almost grotesque little notes of condolence she sometimes wrote to friends. There is one poem, for instance, which is rather literal in its insistent inquiry:

> To know just how he suffered would be dear;
> To know if any human eyes were near
> To whom he could intrust his wavering gaze,
> Until it settled firm on Paradise.

Other questions the poet wants answered are, "To know if he was patient, part content,/ Was dying as he thought, or different," or "Was he afraid, or tranquil?" This increasing preoccupation with and curiosity about death betrays a growing conflict in her mind between faith and doubt. Then of course there are the anecdotes about her notes of condolence, one of which suffices to indicate her turn of mind during this late period of life. She wrote to a friend whose father had died on her wedding-day: "Few daughters have the immortality of a father for a bridal gift." Here again one must in honesty ask a number of questions: is this genuine sympathy, is it simply poor taste, is it selfishness which puts one's thoughts about a subject—and the frank expression of them—before consideration for the bereaved friend? However these questions are answered on this and similar occasions, especially as she grew older and more isolated from the outside world, Emily Dickinson inevitably wrote from herself, and not from any contact with realities, either of poetry or of people.

EMILY DICKINSON AS PARADOX.   The foregoing comments suggest that Emily Dickinson's poetry (along with her letters) is her personality, but further, that the personality is a paradox, an apparent contradiction reflected in poetry. In other words, she manages often to represent opposite extremes. Her perverse secretiveness is at the same time what Conrad Aiken has termed an "unhealthy vanity." As Aiken points out, "It is permissible to suggest that her extreme self-seclusion and secrecy was both a protest and a display—a kind of vanity masquerading as modesty. She became increasingly precious of her person as of her thought. Vanity is in her letters—at the last an unhealthy vanity. She was certainly deprived of such close human relationships as marrying, having her own children, and being in intimate contact with many people. Perhaps this isolation came through a combination of circumstances beginning with her own personality, and was molded in the household of a shrinking mother and a dominating father. At the same time she seems to have been a perfectionist (a quality very much encouraged by the tenets of Calvinism, which assumes that man is born sinful and must forever attempt to perfect himself), inclined to reject people whom she could not understand or communicate with. Indeed, that poem which is so often used to preface anthologies of her poetry is quite characteristic of a familiar quality she reveals, a rather tongue-in-cheek yet injured attitude toward the world. It begins, "This is my letter to the world,/ That never wrote to me, . . ." She is communicating with the world, but without answer.

CONTRADICTIONS.   We have seen that her attitudes toward traditional religion were somewhat schizophrenic—she both believed and disbelieved, which of course is an attitude more natural than unnatural for the inquiring, sensitive mind of any century. Even her poetry must be regarded as contradictory; she can be mystical or trivial, profound or childish. Her techniques have been termed "irresponsible" and "barbarous" by the same critics who praise her power and sometimes frightening insight; she is sometimes original, sometimes commonplace and trite; she has been lauded for preciseness and concision, yet she is often redundant, repeating in the second stanza what was already said in the first. Perhaps these contradictions can be reconciled for the moment in the words of Thomas Wentworth Higginson, writing after her death for a volume of her poems which he helped select. No longer inclined to quarrel with her strange grammar, he put his finger on what is of permanent value in her poetry, saying, "After all, when a thought takes one's breath away, a lesson on grammar seems an impertinence."

THE PUBLISHED POEMS.   The first small volume of Emily Dickinson's poems was brought out in 1890. It was put together by Mabel Loomis Todd, wife of an Amherst professor, and Thomas Wentworth Higginson. Two more volumes, and two volumes of letters as well, soon followed. More poems were published in 1914, and in the twenties. An edition in 1929, titled *Further Poems of Emily Dickinson,* edited by Martha Dickinson Bianchi and Alfred Leete Hampson, is indicative of how much the texts of her poems have been tampered with. The scholar Theodore Spencer bluntly labelled this volume as incompetent. He complained: "Disregarding the most obvious indications of meter and rhyme, they have distorted nearly every poem into an arbitrary shape of their own invention;

what should plainly be one line is printed as two, what should be two is printed as one, until we have an exasperating hybrid which is neither quatrain nor free verse." And unfortunately, in the rush of recognition of Emily Dickinson's worth in the twenties and thereafter, far too many of her poor poems have come into print along with the good. She is a great poet, but any poet who produced 1,775 poems solitarily and without outside criticism cannot be uniformly great. Furthermore, as another of her more recent editors, Robert N. Linscott, observes, there are a number of problems in editing her work: the poems are undated; most of them exist in her handwriting and in fact are usually arranged chronologically according to the striking changes in her script from year to year; she was given to erratic and uncommon punctuation and extensive use of capital letters; and of course her poems were untitled—where we find titles they have come from editors.

HARVARD EDITION.   In 1950 Harvard University bought all available manuscripts and the publishing rights, and issued in 1955 what can be regarded as the definitive (authoritative) edition of her poems and letters in three volumes (sometimes combined into one large volume). This edition by Thomas H. Johnson is often referred to by critics. The most usual and useful method of arrangement in the smaller and handier anthologies is indexing by first lines, as in Robert N. Linscott's Anchor collection, *Selected Poems and Letters of Emily Dickinson,* New York, 1959, where the poems also fall into a roughly chronological order. Another method is the grouping of poems under themes such as Life, Nature, Love, Time and Eternity, as in Conrad Aiken's Modern Library anthology, where identification of each poem is by number, a less functional method. In the analyses below, the poems are considered in a roughly thematic fashion, as in Aiken's anthology; but these groupings are quite arbitrary and overlapping, since a poem on "Nature" may also deal with "immortality," or a presumed "love-poem" may speak of loss by death. The categories that follow are: "Love, Loss, Pain, Despair"; "Time, Death, Immortality"; "Nature"; and "Life, Society."

SUMMARY AND ANALYSIS OF THE POEMS
RENUNCIATION/ IS A PIERCING VIRTUE

This poem amounts to a definition of "renunciation," or going-without, a highly regarded Puritan virtue. Renunciation is defined both literally and in metaphor. What chiefly concerns us here, with this prime example of excellence in Emily Dickinson's poetry, is what has happened to turn a theory or a reflection into poetry. The key, of course, is in the imagination of the poet, for in all ages imagination of the poet has brought about the transformation of personal revelation into poetry. As one well-known critic, R. P. Blackmur, comments, "The puritan theory of renunciation, for example, will be not at all the same thing in a hortatory tract, no matter how eloquent and just, as in a poem of Emily Dickinson, which might well have drawn from the tract. . . . Imagination, if it works at all, works at the level of actualized experience."

IMAGINATIVE LINGUISTIC COMBINATIONS.   Since "actualized experience"—and the way she actualized it—is the absolute key to understanding Emily Dickinson's poetry, the poem in question, so excellently representative of her technique, is reproduced here in full so that we can have it before us word for word:

> Renunciation
> Is a piercing virtue,
> The letting go
> A presence for an expectation—
> Not now.
>
> Rehearsal to ourselves
> Of a withdrawn delight
> Affords a bliss like murder,
> Omnipotent, acute.

16

To return to the idea of "actualized experience," Blackmur goes on to remark that this poem "is the sort of thing that happens to a religious notion when one's awareness of it becomes personal and without authority, when one is driven to imagine—in words or otherwise—the situation actually felt." Notice that the poet has taken one grand concept-word—*renunciation*—then built a striking "image" of it (for if we follow through with each word, we *feel* what renunciation may be like) through the use of stock words and familiar, even colloquial phrases: *letting go, not now, rehearsal.* What is the first word with shock value? *Piercing.*

Piercing has distinct physical connotations which could not escape the reader, and linked with *renunciation,* it demonstrates immediately that there is actual pain connected with renouncing something. Yet, paradoxically but according to the best Puritan ethic, renunciation is said to be a *virtue.* The next words which conjure up a physical image or feeling are *letting go,* which has a familiar colloquial sense and suggests the abrupt release of something held tightly: a person, a thing, pent-up feelings. So, if we are to distort the poem at this point into a kind of dictionary definition, we could say: Renunciation is to let go of "a concrete good for an expectation." In looking back, however, the reader should inquire, why not the word *present,* since we have *expectation?* In other words, especially in Puritan philosophy, give up a present pleasure for promise of a future bliss; or, in more childlike, human terms, give up a present desire for some future and more worthwhile reward. *Presence,* we must thus conclude, is there for a reason, to suggest a person instead of a mere situation. (We recall, of course, that loss of "persons" can be reinforced from what we know of Emily Dickinson's biography.) In any case, *presence, because* it puts a human being in the picture and therefore suggests the real pain of separation from such a human being, is a much more forceful word than *present* would have been. What then is the effect of the *not now* (as well as the punctuating dash that separates it from the four preceding lines? *Not now* is abrupt, clipped, not even a sentence, but it sounds absolute, especially if we imagine it issuing from the disciplining parent. One cannot question that *not now!* and one must, with stubborn but painful reluctance, "let go" of the cherished object. In short, it is the very childlike tone with which "renunciation" is treated that increases its terrors.

DEVELOPMENT.   The second stanza is not a case of redundance (that is, needless repetition) as long as the poet develops the image—which she does. "Rehearsal to ourselves," of course, simply means the dreadful remembering of what has been renounced, the "withdrawn delight." Here again, *rehearsal* is more effective than *remembering* might be, since it suggests going over and over again in one's mind; the pain does not diminish. The shock value in this stanza rests in the word *murder,* which must evoke physical violence, and in the juxtaposition of *bliss* with *murder,* as well as *omnipotent* with *acute. Bliss,* here, may very well mean earthly bliss, but the inevitable association, given the strong hint of the Puritan in *renunciation,* is with heavenly bliss. The reader is surely shaken, then, by the idea that bliss can be like murder, which is certainly "omnipotent" and "acute." (*Acute,* by the way, conects back neatly with *piercing* in its physical connotations.) But then, of course, the reader recalls that the "bliss" referred to here in the second stanza is after all the queer exaltation one may get from "rehearsing" or remembering some painful renunciation. Hence, the paradox: the gratification at having been "virtuous" and the pain of loss, "piercing" pain like "murder," are completely at war in the poem, heightening the effect of both ideas. Much of this effect has been accomplished by original and unexpected word usage.

COMMENT: While there is little doubt that the inspiration for such a poem as this one resides in some personal and painful experience of the poet and that the intensity of Emily Dickinson's feeling probably was a large factor in the excellent poem which resulted, there is an important undercurrent of irony with respect to "the Puritan ethic" which must be pointed out. This irony is similar to other sharp poetic thrusts at the traditional "faith" throughout her poetry; one has been previously cited:

Faith is a fine invention
For gentlemen who see;
But microscopes are prudent
In an emergency!

There is not much doubt, then, that in taking the traditional virtue of "renunciation," throwing in some conventional terminology—*bliss, omnipotent*—then distorting both by the vision of pain she conjures up, Emily Dickinson is very deliberately exploding a myth of her Calvinist upbringing, that it "feels good" to give up things, that renunciation is a virtue which can be easily and automatically practiced.

REMORSE IS MEMORY AWAKE

Probably the second most obsessive theme of Emily Dickinson's, after the theme of death, time and immortality, is that of pain and its various forms. Without a doubt, pain to this poet meant "mental anguish," but it is just as real as physical pain, because of the intensity of her imagination and her constant poetic exploration of this pain. Although we are not sure how or why, we can be certain that this poet suffered. One rich expression of this mental pain, filled with paradoxical word combinations and displaying the poet at her best in terms of conciseness, rhyme and meter, is "Remorse Is Memory Awake." The first stanza reads:

Remorse is memory awake,
Her companies astir,—
A presence of departed acts
At window and at door.

The crowding together of unusual words, particularly in the first two stanzas, makes desirable a combined summary and analysis here. Like the poem "Renunciation is a piercing virtue" (and countless others), the pattern here is to take an abstraction —"remorse"—and make it concrete by the images which the somewhat unorthodox word clusters inspire. Another familiar Dickinsonian device seen in this first stanza is the "humanizing" or "actualizing" of *memory* and of *acts*. Memory is likened to an army, a group, perhaps a household of people, since "remorse is memory awake,/ Her companies *astir,*" as when a household comes awake in the morning. The "departed acts" seem a little ghostly—like bad spirits—but real, since they are present everywhere, "at window and at door." Remorse, then, is not abstract at all, but a collection of live, painful, remembered acts which press upon the consciousness.

In the second stanza the language becomes a little artificial and stiff, especially in the last two lines:

> Its past set down before the soul,
> And lighted with a match,
> Perusal to facilitate
> Of its condensed despatch.

Also, there is not much logical continuity of imagery from first to second (or to third) stanzas; that is, the images here in the second stanza have but remote connection with those of the first. "Its past" (remorse's) is "set down before the soul," in the manner of the daily newspaper, we soon discover; although it is a little awkward to visualize the "perusal" of that "past" ("its condensed despatch") as being much helped by a mere lighted match. Hopefully, the match may stand for a candle or lamp.

The last stanza is rather prosaic, enlivened only by the Puritan idea of remorse as earthly punishment by God, his "complement of hell." Thus she describes remorse to the human being as similar to hell, to the damned soul.

MY LIFE CLOSED TWICE BEFORE ITS CLOSE

If we follow the syntax of Emily Dickinson's best poetry carefully, it reveals itself with a direct simplicity. The first stanza of this poem raises a doubt as to whether a "third event" (the poet's own death) could equal the impact of the double loss referred to as "my life closed twice." This loss, which remains unidentified, seems more "huge" and "hopeless" than would her own death. The last two oft-quoted lines are a deft conclusion, illustrating Dickinson's capacity for a swift, intense "summing up": "Parting is all we know of heaven/ And all we need of hell." Parting, like remorse, is a kind of hell on earth.

> **COMMENT:** The effective last two lines of the poem raise an important question: was the parting caused by death or by separation? Either interpretation is possible, since we know that the poet lost at least two friends of youth through death, and we know that she was doomed to a physical separation from the Reverend Wadsworth with whom she fell in love in the mid-1850's. Since critics generally assume that her most creative and intense poetic output was during the 1860's in the aftermath of her "affair" (which was chiefly an affair of the mind) with this gentleman, the second interpretation is probably preferable: she met him in Philadelphia in 1855, but was separated from him (although there was some correspondence); later she was more permanently separated from him when he left the East and went to preach on the West Coast.

The poem illustrates Dickinson at her poetic best in its fortunate combination of simple but meaningful words. She is not given to multisyllabic words although she falls at times into more quaint, archaic-sounding usages than we find here; in this poem we find the ultra-simplicity of form which is characteristic of her. She most often employs iambic tetrameter lines (4-foot, 8-beat) and alternating rhymes, sometimes off-rhyme (unveil—befell, hell). The first line might be considered awkward in its repetition of *close,* and that too is typical of her poems—when used sparingly, such repetition is successful; when excessive, it can become ineffective. The spirit of anguish is conveyed in the grand sweep of the "so huge, so hopeless to conceive," as well as in the unalterable pronouncement of the last two lines. The idea of parting as a form of dying, in a way more terrible than death because the bereft one knows the other to be alive somewhere but out of reach, is of course a topic of frequent and earnest treatment among poets. Dickinson, however, uses it more often and with a more cutting effect than most poets have.

I NEVER LOST AS MUCH BUT TWICE

The first line, "I never lost as much but twice," suggests, by the phrase "as much," that there is a third loss to be recorded, which we see is the case from the second stanza. The other three lines of the first stanza simply make clear that the first two losses were through death, by reference to "sod" and the "door of God." We infer from the beginning of the second stanza that angels, after "twice descending," "reimbursed" her store by providing another object of admiration or love. But the rapid-fire ending which addresses God as "burglar, banker, father," declares "I am poor once more!"

COMMENT: As mentioned in the Introduction, it is conjectured that the first two losses Emily Dickinson speaks of in the first stanza are her young friends who encouraged her interest in books and in writing poetry, Leonard Humphrey and Benjamin F. Newton, both of whom died young. Her biographers suggest, however, that the third loss developed in the second stanza is a reference to the Reverend Wadsworth, the man she seems really to have loved, and to his departure from the East for a ministerial position in San Francisco.

POETICS.   Form and style need little comment in this poem, since they fall into what must be regarded as typical Dickinson poetics: a three- or four-foot (6 or 8 beat) line, with alternate rhyme. This poem of course contains mostly three-foot lines; the second and fourth lines of each stanza rhyme. The richness of the poem lies in a colloquial quality which Emily Dickinson at her best can achieve: to "stand a beggar before the door of God," for example, is a vivid and homely image, and illustrates her ability to combine the familiar with the mystical or abstract. The subject matter of the poem, in other words, is commonplace, in that it speaks of losing two friends by death, one by separation. But the peculiarly original language enables the reader to *see* a grieving, puzzled girl standing forlornly before a "real" door of God. In short, the "pearly gates" are transformed through excellent choice of words into a credible door on an Amherst street.

WORD USAGE.   The second stanza continues this effective combination of "abstracts" with "concretes." *Angels,* for example, if mentioned alone, would remain abstract, vague, a "concept"; but when they descend to *reimburse* someone, the language of the street and the marketplace—of everyday business transactions—has intervened to make the scene seem very real. This method becomes startling in the line "Burglar, banker, father." It is conventional to address God as *father;* it is unconventional, perhaps irreverent, to call God a *burglar* and a *banker.* These words describe God as one who can take away and give back at his own whim and will; this is similar to a more conventional rendering of the thought "the Lord giveth and the Lord taketh away," which is surely in the background; but the poet's version of it is entirely original.

PAIN HAS AN ELEMENT OF BLANK

The first stanza might be said to reverse the commonplace notion that pain is always acute, since it asserts that pain takes on a numbness and its fluctuations are minute. The second stanza builds on the futility of pain, because "it has no future but itself" and can only look forward to more pain.

> **COMMENT:**   This is a relatively undistinguished poem. Its ordinariness is redeemed, however, by its realization of the experience of "pain," particularly as it conveys the grim futility of that sort of pain which one does not expect to cease. The dullness here could be physical or mental; in any case it is omnipresent. The first line, "Pain has an element of blank," despite the poetic awkwardness of the word *blank,* is effective in introducing what turns out to be a very credible account of the consciousness of pain: "It cannot recollect/ When it began, or if there were/ A day when it was not." There is more power expressed in the futility of the second stanza: pain is pictured as practically feeding upon itself, hence perpetually, damnably renewed:
>
> It has no future but itself,
> Its infinite realms contain
> Its past, enlightened to perceive
> New periods of pain.
>
> It is interesting to note that, although the reader comes away from this poem with the sense of having heard the word *pain* many times repeated, it occurs only twice: as the first and the last words of the poem. Even though this is not one of Emily Dickinson's greatest poems, it is another example of her ability to actualize experience, to concretize abstract ideas.

I CANNOT LIVE WITH YOU

This poem, among her longest, may be ranked among the best of her so-called love poems. Indeed, it comes the nearest to making a credible case for unrequited love, even though it may have been entirely one-sided. It falls into three sections, treating respectively life with the loved one, death with him, and resurrection with him. The first three stanzas assert that "life" with him is out of reach:

> . . . over there
> Behind the shelf
>
> The sexton keeps the key to,
> Putting up
> Our life, his porcelain,
> Like a cup
>
> Discarded of the housewife,
> Quaint or broken;
> A newer Sèvres pleases,
> Old ones crack.

According to these stanzas, the sexton—keeper of the church— has had a hand in keeping the lovers apart; indeed, he has no notion of the importance of "their life," discarding it as a house-wife puts aside cracked china. The next two stanzas (fourth and fifth) insist that she could not die with her lover because, in the natural order of things, one of them would have to precede the other in death and neither of them would be willing to do this:

> For one must wait
> To shut the other's gaze down,—
> You could not.

> And I, could I stand by
> And see you freeze,
> Without my right of frost,
> Death's privilege?

The last section, dealing with resurrection, considers the poet standing before judgment, and for questioning as to whether the judgment would be damnation or salvation. The idolization of the lover is seen in the stanza:

> Nor could I rise with you,
> Because your face
> Would put out Jesus',
> That new grace
>
> Glow plain and foreign
> On my homesick eye,
> Except that you, than he
> Shone closer by.

That is, the grace of the Saviour would pale for her and she would feel "homesick" unless her lover, the shining one, were nearby. The next two stanzas continue to substitute the excellence of the earthly lover for heavenly grace, the poet mentioning that her lover served heaven (a pretty clear hint of the Reverend Wadsworth) although she "could not." She asserts that the reason she could not serve heaven was that her lover obscured in his loveliness that abstract place for her:

> Because you saturated sight,
> And I had no more eyes
> For sordid excellence
> As Paradise.

He filled her gaze, in other words—"saturated sight"—and Paradise became a "sordid excellence." If he were damned, she goes on to say ("and were you lost"), she would have to be damned also, even if her name was famous in heaven. On the

other hand, if he were saved, anywhere she herself was condemned to be, would be hell. Then the inevitable conclusion:

> So we must keep apart,
> You there, I here,
> With just the door ajar
> That oceans are,
> And prayer,
> And that pale sustenance,
> Despair!

TONE. There is really little reason to accuse Emily Dickinson of religious blasphemy either in her time or ours, yet this
poem is intriguing in the way it elevates at every turn the earthly
lover over Christ, God the Father, and heavenly bliss. His face
is so glowing as to "put out Jesus'," whose light would seem
"plain and foreign" to her "homesick eye" were her lover not
near. Two stanzas later she reiterates the same fact of his blind-
ing excellence for her: he saturates sight so that Paradise is
sordid. She would choose rather to be damned than saved, if
that were his fate. And where he is not, is hell.

COMMENT: This poem represents the clearest hint we
have of Emily Dickinson's passion, however isolated and
one-sided it may have been, for her minister friend Wadsworth. The real clues are the word *sexton,* associated with
a keeper of the church and perhaps with authorities of
the church, who would have had a hand in the removal of
Wadsworth to the West Coast. Another indication is in
the lines, "For you served Heaven, you know,/ Or sought
to," which, while they could apply to any pious and rela-
tively orthodox person, reinforce the association with
Wadsworth. Another interesting suggestion is in the last
stanza:

> You there, I here,
> With just the door ajar
> That oceans are. . . .

This is interesting since she was living on the East Coast—
at one ocean's edge—and he, ultimately, at an opposite
ocean, the Pacific, the continent between them represents
"just the door ajar," reinforced by the "you there, I here."

TECHNIQUE.   There are a number of fine effects of
technique here. There is for example an alternation of
regularity and irregularity of meter which represents Dickinson at her best; the lines manage variety without jerki-
ness. Compare the first and second stanzas, for instance:
both have essentially the same pattern of rhythm, yet the
second stanza gives an impression of more irregularity because of word such as "putting up" and "like a cup." Notice the subtle continuation of a sound, which yet is not
always rhyme, from stanza three to five to six to nine, in
the words *pleases, freeze, Jesus, eyes, Paradise.* The sub-
junctive (would, were) is also effective in the sound
pattern.

And were you lost, I would be,
Though my name
Rang loudest
On the heavenly fame.

And were you saved,
And I condemned to be
Where you were not,
That self were hell to me.

The final stanza is a masterpiece of carefully alternated
meters, highly condensed sentence structure, rhyme, off-
rhyme, and suggestive images. The meter breakdown, line
to line, is 3-foot, 2-foot, 3-foot, 2-foot, 1-foot, 3-foot, 2-
foot, with internal variations. In the "beats" of these lines,
the stress does not fall regularly. For example, in line one,
the stress falls thus—"so *we* must *keep apart.*" But in
line two, there is almost equal stress on each of the four

words, and so on the thought: *"You there, I here."* This
line is also evidence of the condensed sentence structure.
As for rhyme and off-rhyme, we have *apart, here, ajar, are,
prayer, despair;* all are different enough to avoid a monotony of sound similarities. "That pale sustenance" is an
effective characterization of the final, impactful word "Despair!" because it conveys with an image the idea that despair, after all, is very little enlivened (colored, made vig-
orous) by hope. This stanza—in fact the entire poem—
is among those which enhance the reputation of Emily
Dickinson.

THE SOUL SELECTS HER OWN SOCIETY

The first stanza of this well-known poem suggests that a "soul,"
or a person (it may be either, as will be seen below) may
choose his "society," and that such a choice is "divine majority," cannot be questioned: "On her divine majority/ Obtrude
no more." In the second stanza the pressures against this choice
are enumerated; but she—the soul, the speaker—remains "unmoved" before "the chariot's pausing/ At her low gate," and
before the "emperor . . . kneeling/ Upon her mat." The third
stanza is reflective commentary, and reiteration of the thought
of the first stanza:

> I've known her from an ample nation
> Choose one;
> Then close the valves of her attention
> Like stone.

LANGUAGE.   By virtue of the Dickinsonian touch in language, the soul emerges as a kind of royal princess in this poem.
She "selects her own soicety," as a princess would do. Her selection of the "suitor" or "prince," we presume, amounts to a
"divine majority" (monarchs, after all, were once considered to
have "divine authority," that is, authority direct from God)
which is absolute: "On her divine majority/ Obtrude no more."

Obtrude is a better word, for example, than *intrude* would be, carrying with it more of the idea of opposition, outside pressures. The theme of royalty is continued in the second stanza, as the *chariot* pauses to solicit her company and the *emperor* himself kneels entreating her "upon her mat," demeaning himself in a quite un-emperorlike manner. The third stanza returns to the picture of royal princes making her selection: "I've known her from an ample nation/ Choose one." Her decision, again, is absolute: the valves of her attention are closed "like stone." *Valves* is another instance of the poet's irresistible insertion of a familiar, workaday term into an otherwise rather "philosophical" statement of policy.

> **COMMENT:**   Since it appears unlikely that Emily Dickinson is retelling one of *Grimm's Fairy Tales* here, let us look for her intended meaning. The poem has often been used as evidence toward the reason for her increased seclusion after losing the love of the Reverend Wadsworth. If so, it is the stubborn and somewhat narrow-minded withdrawal of a rather petulant, perfectionist "soul," or self, who was perhaps rather timorous of life to begin with. But there is another possible way of looking at this poem: as an expression of Emily Dickinson's refusal throughout her life to espouse formally the Orthodox Church—Trinitarian Congregationalist—of her community and her fellows. In this interpretation the images of royalty are still valid, here pertaining to the orthodox traditions of the Church and the traditional concept of an omnipotent God. Her announcement that her choice is final, absolute, indicates that she firmly believed in and would thus adhere to her own version of Christianity, which is strongly based in earthly matters, in nature, in her own minutely investigated consciousness of things.

SUPERIORITY TO FATE

This too is a poem of deprivation, and how one learns to deal with it. The poet says (first stanza) that it is not conferred but earned, as we learn from the second stanza, "a pittance at a time." In such a gradual way the soul learns, though deprived, to "subsist" in life until Paradise.

> **COMMENT:** Although representing Emily Dickinson in its excellence of preciseness, this poem is just another example of a life philosophy grounded in pessimism, Puritan pessimism which stresses the "vale of tears" over happinesses in the earthly life. The poet is saying that fate has dealt her a hard blow but she has learned with difficulty to be toughminded. Furthermore, it is bad enough to have to "rise above" a sorry fate ("superiority to fate") but one also has to "earn" it: another Puritan ideal, hard-wrought rewards through sweat and tears and self-denial. And this "worker" toiling toward "superiority to fate" is paid shockingly little—he rises "a pittance at a time," like a slave, perhaps increasing his subservience to God or that fate. However disappointed in life he has been, if he lives frugally he will manage to subsist to his death, which by implication here is a release:

Until, to her surprise,
The soul with strict economy
Subsists till Paradise.

This is a powerful but somewhat grotesque poem, in the sense that it betrays such a shrunken, circumscribed vision of life.

IT WAS NOT DEATH, FOR I STOOD UP

This poem is describing a state or condition which is like death, although it is built on the series of statements that the state is *not* death: "It was not death, for I stood up,/ And all the dead lie down." In fact the occasion of the poem was the high point of the day, literally or figuratively: "for all the bells/ Put out their tongues . . ." It is customary to herald the noon hour with bells. The second stanza insists it was not "frost," as in death, "for on my flesh/ I felt siroccos crawl" (the sirocco is a hot, oppressive wind). Yet the speaker "freezes" too, for her "marble feet/ Could keep a chancel cool" (the chancel is the rail or lattice which separates the altar area from the rest of the church). But the premise of the poem is stated in the first line of the third stanza: "And yet it tasted like them all." She then describes in stanzas three and four how her body and her self feel dead, numb, like "the figures I have seen/ Set orderly, for burial."

> As if my life were shaven
> And fitted to a frame,
> And could not breathe without a key;
> And 'twas like midnight, some. . . .

The first three lines of this stanza are suggestive of the preparation of the body for burial, stripping it of the elements of life toward a final confinement. This "condition," she goes on to discuss in the fifth stanza, is also a little like ("some") midnight, "when everything that ticked has stopped." *Ticked,* it would seem refers to the ticking off of all the activities of the day as well as to the implication that the clock stops ticking, in other words, it refers to silence . . . and "staring" space all around, or emptiness. Or the state of the speaker is likened unto "first autumn morns," when "grisly frosts . . . repeal the beating ground." The most plausible explication of this line—*repeal* and *beating* are words that give some trouble of interpretation— seems to be that the first frosts of autumn, that is, hints of hardening winter to come, cancel out the ground which was formerly pulsating or throbbing ("beating") with life. But, the final stanza asserts, the condition was most like "chaos, stopless, cool. . . "; like floating in a vacuum, "without a chance or spar,/ Or even a report of land/ To justify despair." The concluding imagery suggests an endless sea—"stopless"—where, para-doxically, since there is no hope, neither is there despair.

COMMENT: As one critic, Austin Warren, has pointed out, Emily Dickinson is at her most powerful in the poems which suggest by negation; that is, what she insists something is *not* like, it *is* like, and we have another poem about death-in-life. She is among the "walking dead." In its five stanzas this poem actually builds on its horrors; it is more terrible, for instance, to feel dead at high noon, the peak of day, than it would be at midnight. The second stanza, with its contrasts of frost and fire which the speaker feels, suggests the traditional miserable state of the lover pictured in Elizaethan love sonnets: "I freeze, I burn." The two middle stanzas, as mentioned above, liken the condition to that of a body being prepared for burial. "Could not breathe without a key" reiterates and increases the horror of suffocation suggested by the "siroccos," those hot, stifling winds. *Lifelessness* is the keynote throughout: midnight is the technical end of the day, emphasized here by the imagined stopping of the clocks. "Space stares, all around," suggesting a wide and lifeless sea, an idea continued in the last stanza; and the ground is frozen, without further hope of life. A person surrounded by chaos which is stopless and cool is like a person adrift in space, a space of sea or of air or vacuum.

LANGUAGE. The figurative language employed here, then, although it is mixed, all converges on the central idea of death-in-life, or, as Austin Warren suggests, the stanzas progressively construct the sense of a self being "de-animized," the life being taken from it, ending with the ultimate desolation, like the state of Dante's souls in limbo in *The Inferno*. Because there is no hope, neither chance nor spar nor report of land, there is no despair, and vice versa.

JUST ONCE—OH LEAST REQUEST!

Another of Emily Dickinson's poems of personal deprivation, although not nearly so eloquent as "I asked no other thing," or even "Superiority to fate," this is a kind of bewildered outburst against God. The first stanza emphasizes how small the poet's request must have seemed before the grandeur of the Almighty and the multitude of claims presented to Him—"So small a grace,/ So scanty put." The second stanza puzzles on:

> Would not a God of flint
> Be conscious of a sigh,
> As down his heaven dropt remote,
> "Just once, sweet Deity?"

The question, in essence, is why God does not hear and answer one small request.

> **COMMENT:**   As suggested above, the poem is an out-burst—with a poignancy—against the "adamant" God who seems to deny the desperately desired love object. It is this love object for which "Being" is offered. We immediately detect that interpretation admits several possibilities as to the love object: the lost lover, or even one meeting with him, or the promise of immortality or at least some answer to a doubt. "God of flint" is another evidence of Dickinson's conditioning to the stern, judging, Old Testament, Puritan God; but her naiveté inquires whether even such a strict God could not hear a sigh and a childlike plea, "Just once, sweet Deity?" The poem illustrates a personal yet puzzled and unabashed relationship between Emily Dickinson and her God.

I ASKED NO OTHER THING

By the metaphor of the "mighty merchant" Dickinson constructs another poem of suggestion by denial, a monument to the perversity of life. The "buyer" asks but one thing and offers an ultimate price: Being. The merchant smiles, much as we might imagine a dealer in antiques or rare items, mysterious, remote, yet prepared to bargain—except if the customer asks for the impossible.

Brazil? He twirled a button.
Without a glance my way:
"But, madam, is there nothing else
That we can show to-day?"

COMMENT: Quaint. Terrifying. A critical risk, but
these are the terms that apply to this little masterpiece of
pathos and irony. So many of the typical qualities of
Emily Dickinson are in it: brevity (abrupt, almost stilted
sentences); that inevitable homely, familiar locale (here,
the powerful merchant, a customer's desire for the exotic, an indifferent and perverse refusal); at the same time,
the customary inclusion of "abstracts" (here, "Being";
other examples have been *remorse, Paradise, renunciation,
soul*); two words only that rhyme—but the rest tease each
other with kindred sounds (*denied/ smiled; way/ today;
other thing, no other, nothing*). Suggestion by denial,
which we have seen to be an habitual approach for this
poet, means couching in the negative rather than the positive. She does not say, "I asked but one thing"; she says:

I asked no other thing,
No other was denied.

This emphasizes the point that in a world full of things (or,
possibly, people), she wanted one, and that one thing or
person was important enough to offer her whole self for.
With ultimate perversity, it was denied by the mighty
merchant. But here is the power of the poem: the poet has
transformed it by choosing what was to her (and in that
era) a most remote but real country—Brazil—to symbolize this unattainable thing. She has also grounded the
flight of fancy by engaging her imaginary but real merchant
in a natural, mundane, yet terribly significant gesture, since
it belies his own recognition of the terrible importance of
his customer's request: "He twirled a button./ Without a
glance my way. . . ." As readers we feel the pause and the

pull, the maddening moment of hope and question. Does he have it in stock? Will he make an offer? Will he bargain? Then the cruel turn of the screw: "But, madam, is there nothing else/ That we can show to-day?" "Madam," as if she were any other rich patroness with any little, indifferent request; "we" in a cool, corporate sense, as if to shift off any responsibility for denying her, and to assure his detachment from the things he sells.

SIGNIFICANCE.   What was it the poet "asked"? Love, most probably; and perhaps, specifically, the love of the man she believed herself in love with. But the importance of the poem is that it conveys the piercing terror of such a denial; it makes concrete a feeling, makes an experience real to another, conveys an emotion through language. There is a directness, an immediacy here which is Emily Dickinson's greatest power, and which yet somehow eludes analysis, as a great many critics willingly testify.

BECAUSE I COULD NOT STOP FOR DEATH

This poem, sometimes editorially titled "The Chariot," speaks of death in terms of familiar earthly objects. In the first stanza, Death comes as the "kindly" driver of a carriage and stops to pick up the speaker. They ride alone, except for "Immortality" which may be construed as a passenger or an idea, or both. The second stanza describes the ride as leisurely—"he knew no haste." Nor is the passenger in a hurry, having put away both labor and leisure, out of politeness toward Death, "for his civility." The third stanza observes certain items of everyday life, as they pass children playing in a schoolyard, and fields of "grazing grain." It is a turning point in the poem when, in the last line of this third stanza, they pass the "setting sun." The "house" referred to in the first line of the fourth stanza turns out to be, of course, a grave, as evidenced in "a swelling of the ground" and "the cornice but a mound." The last stanza leaps forward in time—"Since then 'tis centuries"—and closes on an affirmative note by indicating that eternity seems short—that is, pleasurable—rather than doomlike. To mention the "horses' heads" is to return, structurally, to the idea of the chariot.

COMMENT: This is one of Emily Dickinson's best and most famous poems, centering upon her obsessive theme of life and immortality. That the poem is grounded in mortal objects is quite clear, from the carriage with driver to the children playing, fields of grain, setting sun, house; yet all these terms serve symbolically too. The children suggest youth, the grain means growth to a ripening, and the setting sun of course is time, and an ending. It may be that the poet is speculating on the literal journey in a hearse to the cemetery, or on the experience of dying, during which there might be reflection on the items of life mentioned. The last stanza is an abrupt change, since it attempts to comment on the nature of the afterlife. The poem is a paradox—and very typical of Emily Dickinson's way of looking at things—because the poet is unable to discuss death except in terms of what she knows of life, or to describe lifelike objects without an undertone of passing time and lack of permanence.

ALLEN TATE.   It is worthwhile to note the differing comments of two critics on what is widely regarded as one of Emily Dickinson's finest poems. Allen Tate calls it "one of the perfect poems in English," illustrating very well the poet's "special quality" of mind. Tate says that "every image is precise and, moreover, not merely beautiful, but fused with the central idea." As for the driver, Death, he thinks that "the terror of death is objectified through this figure of the genteel driver, who is made ironically to serve the end of Immortality. This is the heart of the poem: she has presented a typical Christian theme in its final irresolution. . . ." In other words, Tate praises the poem in all-encompassing (but rather vague) terms. He makes one very interesting observation, though, about Death, that "gentleman taking a lady out for a drive," for this is certainly the note struck by Dickinson with the words "kindly" and "civility." This note is, as Tate rightly points out, a "subtly interfused erotic motive, which the idea of death has presented to most romantic poets, love being a symbol interchangeable with death." It is quite valid to suggest such an erotic note as present in Emily Dickinson's personalized relations with God, especially in view of her deprivation of the human love relationship between man and woman.

YVOR WINTERS.   Yvor Winters is just as admiring but perhaps a little more qualified in his praise of the poem as one of her finest. His most valid point is that the poem is more effective in evoking the life left behind than in its attempt to visualize death and the life to come. He argues, "In the last stanza there is the semi-playful pretense of familiarity with the posthumous experience of eternity, so that the poem ends unconvincingly though gracefully, with a formulary gesture very roughly comparable to that of the concluding couplet of many an Elizabethan sonnet of love; for the rest of the poem is a remarkably beautiful poem on the subject of the daily realization of the imminence of death—it is a poem of departure from life, an intensely conscious leave-taking. In so far as it concentrates on the life that is being left behind, it is wholly successful; in so far as it attempts to experience the death to come, it is fraudulent, however exquisitely, and in this it falls below her finest achievement."

TO KNOW JUST HOW HE SUFFERED WOULD BE DEAR

The first stanza simply asks, did he suffer much in dying, and was there a human friend near to keep him company until he was secure in Paradise? The second stanza continues such literal inquiry into his (the "his" remaining anonymous throughout, as is customary with Emily Dickinson) patience, his "partial content," whether dying was like or unlike what he had expected, and if the day was pleasant and sunny—"Did the sunshine face his way?" Furthermore, in stanza three the poet wonders whether he thought more of God and his future life or of the present earthly life, of home and what his friends, "the distant," would say when they received the news of his death—"that he ceased human nature/ On such a day." The fourth stanza is a little more complicated, because of idiosyncrasies of language; the poet chooses, without apparent design, to add an extra line to the fourth and the sixth stanzas. Again, these are among the common eccentricities of Emily Dickinson, for better or for worse. She wonders if he had wishes, because all that was "legible" to her, the apparent watcher, was his "sigh, accented." Was he confident in hope of heaven until the moment when he departed life? That is, when "ill," was his illness replaced by "everlasting well," his heavenly eternity? The fifth stanza, among the poorest, poetically, and rather superfluous, simply asks, what names did he speak, or half-speak, "at the drowsiest" (nearest to death)? And finally, was he fearful or easy in his mind? The implied answer, in the again somewhat complicated language and syntax of the last stanza, is that he *could* have been tranquil if he realized that the consciousness expands at the moment of death to absorb all the past and present ("love that was") and the promise of God's heavenly love and life ("love too blest to be") into a "meeting" or "junction," which is Eternity.

COMMENT: This poem, which is not necessarily a "good" one, is included as illustrative of Emily Dickinson's growing obsession later in life with death and dying. As suggested above, it appears that her personal conflicts about the traditional Calvinist view of religion, with its assurance of immortality for the virtuous, and what her practical observations of real life offered her, increased as she grew older, unduly emphasized no doubt by her sequestered life of observation and introspection rather than participation. As we know, it was customary at that time.

and still is, among many sects and many families, to "sit up" with the dying and with the dead. Countless items of correspondence and poetry indicate that this Emily Dickinson often did, or that she knew of many people who did it; thus she had more and more occasion to dwell morbidly on the subject of death. This poem, which is in fact a series of almost frowning, childlike questions on death, is typical of her train of thought in the later years. And, like the two who died for beauty and truth and discuss the matter as they lie in separate graves, the situation of this poem is somewhat unpleasant. Such curiosity, although ruthlessly realistic (that is, representative of what might certainly enter the mind of any intelligent and sensitive person), is also morbid. As Conrad Aiken describes it, "Her eagerness for details, after the death of a friend—the hungry desire to know *how* she died—became almost vulture-like."

TECHNIQUE.   No doubt this poem would be ranked among those most "barbarous" or "irresponsible" in technique, with its irregular meter and rhyme and the especially "spasmodic" fifth and seventh stanza. No real pattern of rhyme or off-rhyme (*until, well; best, first, drowsiest*) can be detected. The first two stanzas are awkward in their "sameness" of structure (*To know, to know, to whom. . . . To know*) and in a monotony of iambic tetrameter, 4-foot, 8-beat lines. The worst stanza, because it lacks the quaintness or intricacy of language and syntax which salvages, the fifth, or the last, is the sixth:

And if he spoke, what name was best,
What first,
What one broke off with
At the drowsiest?

As pointed out, the off-rhymes are ineffective, especially the multisyllabic *drowsiest*. The second line is too awk-

wardly short, the third line merely ugly in terms of sound
—"broke off with." This stanza is also a good example
of what can be called "prosaic" in poetry, and legitimately
complained of: that is, because of a combination of all
the defects cited above, the stanza is more like prose than
poetry.

LANGUAGE. The use of language here is worth commenting on, however, since it illustrates Emily Dickinson's
idiosyncrasies which are often used to good advantage.
The word *legible* in the fourth stanza, for example, when
the reader would normally expect *audible,* related to the
word *sigh,* suggests her method of reversals or substitu-
tions of the unexpected, usually with the effect of capturing
the reader's attention. The same principle is exhibited in
the following lines of stanza four: "And was he confident
until/ Ill fluttered out in everlasting well?" There is, first
of all, the juxtaposition of *until/ ill,* combined with an off-
rhyme, *well.* But let us explore what the reader might expect, conventionally, from the thought of this line, which
suggests the common idea that at death all pain naturally
ceases and the soul departs the body. We might expect,
then, that the *soul* should "flutter out"; also, the word
everlasting is traditionally combined with *will.* This makes
for a rather ingenious line, with the word *well* doing double
duty: it suggests well-being or the absence of pain (*ill*) and
at the same time evokes by association the everlasting *will*
of God or everlasting peace of heaven.

The final stanza contains some clever effects with words,
too.

Might he know
How conscious consciousness could grow,
Till love that was, and love too blest to be,
Meet—and the junction be Eternity?

There is the teasing phrase "How conscious consciousness could grow," which could be interpreted syntactically two ways. *Conscious* could be an adjective modifying *consciousness;* this, however, results in a redundancy (repetition of the same thought) that is a little too precious even for Emily Dickinson. More practically, restoring a more natural word order to the sentence, we could say, "Might he know that consciousness could grow more conscious?" —in other words, more *aware?* The second interpretation is more plausible than the first, suggesting that the dying man's consciousness is intensified at this moment, and his greater awareness shows him how human love and divine love converge. *Junction* is another homely or somewhat unorthodox word, evocative of, say, a country crossroads rather than unearthly revelations. Furthermore, sound effects—especially *t* and *e* sounds repeated—enhance the poetic quality of these two lines: "*T*ill love tha*t* was, and love *t*oo bles*t t*o *be,/ Mee*t*—and the junction *be Et*erni*t*y?"

I NEVER SAW A MOOR

We might say that the first stanza of this poem exists for the sake of the premise of the second stanza: heather and waves are real, even though the poet proclaims not to have actually seen either; by the same token God and heaven may be proved, even though they may never be seen.

COMMENT: This is the other side of Emily Dickinson's "religious thought," even if it may represent a little whistling in the dark. In other words, it is at least a cautious expression of faith, faith in things "unseen." This is an example of the "intuitive" faith of the 19th century Transcendentalists like Ralph Waldo Emerson, to whom Emily Dickinson's thought has sometimes been likened. The Transcendentalists stressed a belief in what could not be seen or touched. The first stanza suggests faith which is in evidence from hearsay, the poet implying she has heard about heather and waves and can believe because of what she has heard. If this be so, then there are the more important "truths" of the second stanza, the facts of God and heaven, which can also be intuited from the world.

Notice how personal is Emily Dickinson's relationship with God and heaven: "I never spoke with God,/ Nor visited in heaven," she says, as if heaven were a nearby community and God a neighbor. This is why it is doubtful if we should accuse her of flippancy in such poems as "I never lost as much but twice," where she addresses God as "burglar, banker, father"; for it is likely that according to her method of concretizing everything—stating abstractions in familiar, everyday terms—such a direct relationship with God was natural. What seems whimsical or flippant in her terminology was inevitable in her habits of language and thought. This does not negate, however, the fact that some of her poems are ironic and doubtful about the traditional Calvinist tenets of her time. The popularity of this poem, though, evidences the charm readers find in such an expression of faith.

NOTE ON THE LANGUAGE.   This poem offers an opportunity to return to the problem of various editions of Emily Dickinson's poetry. As mentioned in the Introduction, the definitive edition of her poems is now that in three volumes done by Thomas H. Johnson, first issued in 1955. Reference to this edition (and it is highly recommended to the serious student of her poetry) illuminates certain significant differences in texts of the poems, since some earlier editors, such as Mrs. Bianchi, had substituted or revised where they were not sure of the manuscripts. Professor Johnson, for example, now substitutes the word *checks* for the more usually printed word *chart* in the last stanza of this poem. His justification is a statement from Emily Dickinson's prose, reading, "My assurance of existence of Heaven is as great as though, having surrendered my

checks [tickets] to the conductor, I knew that I had ar-
rived there." Thus, while *chart* means a map, *checks* means
tickets, and this is a significant difference in meaning in the
last stanza of the poem; since to buy a ticket for a distant
place and to surrender one's tickets to the conductor certainly indicate one's faith in the promise of arrival at the
destination.

IT CAN'T BE SUMMER—THAT GOT THROUGH

Apparently a "nature poem," its first stanza seems to suggest
anticipations of autumn and winter—"that long town of white
to cross"—by ruling out or negating summer, "that got through,"
and spring, "it's early yet for spring." There is the perverse use
of *blackbirds,* however, which are hardly harbingers of spring;
the readers expect "robins," conventionally. The second stanza
is similarly perverse: there is no certainty until the third line—
"so sunset shuts my question down"—that the poet was speaking of the day's end in the first two lines: "It can't by dying,
—it's too rouge,—/ The dead shall go in white." The reference
here is both to seasons of the year and seasons of the day.

COMMENT:

It can't be summer,—that got through;
It's early yet for spring;
There's that long town of white to cross
Before the blackbirds sing.

It can't be dying,—it's too rouge,—
The dead shall go in white.
So sunset shuts my question down
With clasps of chrysolite.

The negative approach is the same here as in the poem
"It was not death, for I stood up" suggestion by negation
—"It can't be summer. . . . It can't be dying. . . ." Color

figures largely in unearthing the real meaning, or the multiple meanings of the poem: white, black, rouge, chrysolite (green-yellow, probably referring here to a topaz-like semiprecious stone). We have said that literally the poem implies that because it can't be summer, which is past, or spring, which is yet to come, there is the long winter yet to be got through. "Long town of white to cross" certainly implies a long journey. It was also pointed out that "it can't be dying,—it's too rouge," is misleading, a reference to some conflict in the poet's mind as to what life or death should look like. *Sunset* seems to prove she was merely speaking of the dying day, yet with inquiry as to why it looks so alive—"rouge," "chrysolite," if it is "dead." Actually, though, the sunset does not resolve her question; it merely "shuts it down"—again, a colloquial phrase, as of shutting down a lid or a window.

There is strong suggestion, then, based on certain ambiguous lines in the poem, that it is more than a nature poem: it is a metaphor for something else the poet has on her mind. The metaphor in fact seems to be again the theme of "life-in-death." The significant lines are "There's that long town of white to cross/ Before the blackbirds sing," and "The dead shall go in white." Austin Warren is illuminating in his interpretation of the whiteness: "The reference to white suggests Emily's own habitual garb from this time on. In the Orient, as she may have known, white is the color of lovers who have come through great tribulation and washed their robes. . . . White is the color for her kind of death-in-life. . . ." Red, incidentally, is the Chinese color of "happiness." Interpreting thus, we see that Emily Dickinson was a "dead" who went in white; we know that after 1862, with her increasing seclusion, she dressed entirely in white. And this poem would indicate that she went so because she was a "lover" who had been through "tribulation." As readers we may either attribute this tribulation to the conjectured loss of her fantasized love for Wadsworth, or to other real and imagined losses throughout her life. With such an analysis, the "long town of white to cross" symbolizes her own life, to be lived out in that kind of life-in-death, "before the blackbirds sing," blackbirds being a conventional symbol for death.

THERE'S A CERTAIN SLANT OF LIGHT

One of the most exquisite poems produced by Emily Dickinson, it embodies three recurrent themes: life, death and nature. It is also smoothly fluent in rhyme and meter. The first stanza tries to explain an atmosphere of depression that comes with a late winter afternoon:

> There's a certain slant of light
> On winter afternoons,
> That oppresses, like the weight
> Of cathedral tunes.

Note that immediately there is established a connection between the natural phenomenon—a dying winter afternoon—and something possibly religious—"cathedral tunes." This connection is continued in the second stanza with the statement that this "light" gives us "heavenly hurt" although "we can find no scar." Rather, as the last two lines of the second stanza indicate— "But internal difference/ Where the meanings are"—this hurt is deep, perhaps soul-deep, where things really matter. The somewhat ambiguous first line of the third stanza, "None may teach it anything," suggests that this hurt, this scar, is absolute: one cannot argue with the image—the "slant of light"—or the feeling it produces within oneself:

> 'Tis the seal, despair,—
> An imperial affliction
> Sent us of the air.

"Seal" also suggests absoluteness of the quality defined, "despair," as does the word "imperial" which, by the line "sent us of the air," implies God. The last stanza returns to evoke the slant of light again:

> When it comes, the landscape listens,
> Shadows hold their breath;
> When it goes, 'tis like the distance
> On the look of death.

This whole stanza is suggestive of a moment in time, which is indeed how the everchanging light of sunrise or sunset must be regarded—look away for an instant and the light is altered. Thus there is conveyed in the last stanza an atmosphere of holding one's breath, a suspended quality: "The landscape listens,/ Shadows hold their breath" (for when the light goes, so go the shadows—they "die"). When the light goes, says the poet, it is as if there might not be another day: " 'Tis like the distance/ On the look of death."

> **COMMENT:**   Why, as postulated above, is this a poem about nature, life and death? The winter light is a metaphor for death. Notice how neatly the structure assists in this interpretation, with "light" in the first line and "death" the last word of the poem. One of the beauties of this poem is that it is tightly structured, carefully metered and rhymed; it is a rare instance of idea, image and technique working together for utmost success. The whole poem is a metaphor of "change" in life, or rather the inevitable progress through life to its ending. It is this conviction that really assaults the poet: the winter light means to her, through insight or intuition, the eventual end of her own life. As Yvor Winters explains it, these stanzas "deal with the inexplicable fact of change, of the absolute cleavage between successive states of being . . . seasonal change is employed as the concrete symbol of the moral change. . . . It is rather a legitimate and traditional form of allegory, in which the relationships between the items described resemble exactly

the relationships between certain moral ideas or experiences. . . ." This correspondence between natural phenomena and the life cycle—similarities between nature and man, and the revelation by intuition of divine matters—is precisely what Ralph Waldo Emerson, the leading spokesman of American Transcendentalism, set forth in his famous "Bible" of Transcendentalism, a long essay called "Nature." His disciple and friend, also a Transcendentalist, Henry David Thoreau, asserted the same credo in his writings, especially the familiar *Walden:* through nature we intuit about life and God. Emily Dickinson of course knew the work and stature of Emerson, her contemporary, and may well be influenced here by his thought; this is a much less important point, however, than her expression of her own ideas about change, which are quite different from anything produced by Emerson or Thoreau.

To return to Winters' remarks about the "inexplicable fact of change," we discover how perfectly the language reinforces this interpretation. For instance, the question which surely arose in the reader's mind about the choice of "*cathedral* tunes" is now answerable: not only does *cathedral* establish that there is a religious or mystical significance in the poem, but the fact that the winter light "oppresses, *like* the weight/ Of cathedral tunes" means that hymns, too, oppress the speaker. The cathedral tunes, while they are beautiful as the winter light, are also sadly evocative of deeper reflections. Similarly, the winter light gives "heavenly hurt" because it is suggestive of deeper thoughts; this is evidenced by the phrase, "internal difference/ Where the meanings are"; it is the *soul* that is hurt or scarred, changed by this mysterious late afternoon fading light. The third stanza simply re-emphasizes the absoluteness of this deep soul-conviction brought on by the light. That the conviction is one of the impermanence of life and the certainty of death is brought out by the figurative reference to God ("imperial") and to heaven ("sent us of the air").

In relation to the last stanza, which is probably one of the best Emily Dickinson ever produced, it is relevant to quote another woman poet, Adelaide Crapsey. Almost a contemporary of Dickinson, she wrote poetry which in its brevity, concision and imagery has been compared to hers. A short poem on the identical theme of change reveals, like Dickinson's, how inevitable, yet imperceptible, yet absolute change is:

These be
Three silent things:
The falling snow, the hour
Before the dawn, the mouth of one
Just dead.

Both poets have captured the imperceptible yet pathetically absolute nature of natural and human change, with mystical overtones. As that late winter afternoon light comes and goes, all the world around and the introspective speaker "hold their breath," actually in dread of the change when the light is gone. This dread—the "oppression" of the first stanza—is borne out by the bleakness of the last lines: "When it goes, 'tis like the distance/ On the look of death"—a distance which, insofar as the observer is concerned, is also absolute and unending. Two other poems, also among Dickinson's best, are in a similar vein, injecting the quality of pathos and mysticism into seasonal change. These are "A light exists in spring. . ." and "As imperceptibly as grief. . ."

AS IMPERCEPTIBLY AS GRIEF

The excellence of this poem competes with "There's a certain slant of light," and, like that poem, it represents Emily Dickinson at her best on the subject of nature. Sometimes she can be trite, trivial or childishly simplified with nature subjects but here she is not. Perhaps the key to the greatness of both poems is in the additional thematic overtones they offer, for life and death—time—are their topics, as well as nature. To say that the first stanza states how "imperceptibly" the summer passed—which it does—is proof of how ridiculous it sometimes seems to paraphrase Emily Dickinson's poetry; for when she is not being purposely obscure or confusing—and sometimes incomprehensible or even meaningless—her subjects are directly and immediately revealed. It is the manner in which she thinks and the technique which she selects to express her thought that invariably require analysis. This poem elaborates on the growing sensation that summer is ending. In stanza two, there is a "quietness," growing partly out of the earlier twilight as the days are shorter; stanza three says in effect that the morning now comes later too; the last stanza simply observes that the summer has slipped away.

COMMENT: While there is no metaphor for death in this poem (as in "There's a certain slant of light"), there is the pervasive theme of change and the passage of time; and, if there is a note of pathos, it is that this slipping away of time is so imperceptible. Loosely speaking, the summer symbolizes the fullness of life; this makes more understandable the simile using "grief" in the first stanza:

As imperceptibly as grief
The summer lapsed away,—
Too imperceptible, at last,
To seem like perfidy.

Grief is a useful comparison anyway, of course, since any reader's human experience would verify that grief, however painful at first, does slip away gradually in almost unnoticed departure. But to juxtapose grief with summer is to encourage the association with sadness; hence a note of pathos in the first stanza. If we carry the metaphor of summer as "life" into the third and fourth lines, the sadness pervades there, too. *Perfidy* is the choice and meaningful

word—that is, one would like to lament how the summer
—life—slips away, but it happens so gradually that it
cannot be accounted a betrayal.

THEMES.   The thematic progress of the second stanza
is enriched by two words, especially: *distilled* and *sequestered.* "Slow change" and "silence" emerge from this
second stanza, for distillation is of course a time-consum-
ing process, and quietness is here distilled. We note also
Dickinson's typical injection of the everyday word *distilled* into the discussion of something natural yet mysterious and sad. Pathos is increased in this second stanza by
a rather graceful personification of Nature, seen as "spending with herself/ Sequestered afternoon" (a circumstance
so familiar to the poet herself). The inverted sentence
structure of the first two lines of stanza three is also
effective:

The dusk drew earlier in,
The morning foreign shone,—
A courteous, yet harrowing grace,
As guest who would be gone.

While it is the conventional practice of all poets so to distort and compact their sentences, it is particularly lovely
here, combined as it is with fortunate sound effects (*d*'s,
n's, *r*'s). *Harrowing* is perhaps the most original touch in
this stanza, much more vivid for example than "hurrying"
would be, since it implies both disarray and restlessness on
the part of the "guest," and this pressured mood passed
on to the "host." *Harrowing,* after all, usually is taken to
mean distressing, vexing, uncomfortable—hence a mutual
distress is conveyed. Again, a personification of morning
as "guest" further illustrates Emily Dickinson's habitual
and soundly poetic impulse to make "abstracts" (morning,
nature; elsewhere, death) concrete and humanized. Or, as
we put it previously, this is another example of her ability

to actualize experience. There is a question, or at least an ambiguity of punctuation, in this stanza:

The morning foreign shone,—
A courteous, yet harrowing grace,
As guest who would be gone.

One might read "the morning foreign shone" with a pause or a period, since the idea is that the mornings come later and later as autumn sets in. On the other hand, the lines could easily read, "The morning foreign shone a courteous, yet harrowing grace, as guest who would be gone"—in other words, the morning is also showing, politely, the wish to be on its way, to shorten more and more its duration. As long as we are playing with punctuation—and it is all too necessary, given the manuscripts of Emily Dickinson's poetry—we could also suggest, with the second punctuation: "The morning, foreign, shone a courteous. . . ."

Like the "light escape" it comments on, the last stanza is the lightest and the weakest, because of the descent to the prosaic in the last line, "Into the beautiful." The lines, "And thus, without a wing,/ Or service of a keel," are vivid enough, suggesting again the imperceptible, invisible transport from summer into autumn. There is no visible means of transport here, no keel (the main center frame of a ship, or the ship itself). For some reason—perhaps a wish to subjectify the summer—the poet chooses to say "our summer" instead of "the summer." Notice too that in the second and fourth lines of each stanza the end words are more carefully and effectively off-rhymed than usual: away, perfidy; begun, afternoon; shone, gone; keel, beautiful. The fact remains, though, that the closing line is weak and falls a little flat.

Yvors Winters' summary comment on this poem, along with the "There's a certain slant of light," and "A light exists in spring," is appropriate. He commends their "directness, dignity, and power . . . the quality of the phrasing, at once clairvoyant and absolute," which raises them "to the highest level of English lyric poetry."

IT MAKES NO DIFFERENCE ABROAD

Ostensibly a nature poem—or more accurately, a poem centered in nature—its first and second stanzas establish how things of nature seem to go on in the face of happenings in the outside world. In the first stanza, the seasons, the days, blossom as always; in the second, wild-flowers and brooks and blackbirds go along in their usual, natural way. The last stanza and the last line of the second—"for passing Calvary"—finally give a hint of the point of the poem: judgments seem to have little meaning for the bee, who suffers only from separation from the rose.

> **COMMENT:** More than one poet has of course observed the continuing cycle of nature in the face of stupendous personal or public events. This seems to be the core of thought here, too: "*It* makes no difference abroad, whatever "it" is. Accustomed as we are to Emily Dickinson's mode of thought and expression, we can guess she is referring to a private event: one of her losses of a friend by death, or the separation from Wadsworth or some other idealized love figure.

> There are some nice effects of language in this poem. In the first stanza,

> The mornings blossom into noons,
> And split their pods of flame,

> a neat association of the season of the day (noon/flame) with the "season" of the wild-flowers in the second stanza continues the fire image and the sense of life to good advantage. This quality of aliveness is reinforced in the incessant noise of the brooks and the blackbird:

The brooks brag all the day;
No blackbird bates his jargoning
For passing Calvary.

(*Bates* means abates, reduces.)

Calvary, with its inevitable association with the crucifixion
of Christ, at least implies sacrifice or loss, perhaps death,
an idea borne out in the last stanza:

Auto-da-fé and judgment
Are nothing to the bee;
His separation from his rose
To him seems misery.

Auto-da-fé is a term to be explored for its ambiguous pos-
sibilities. Taken literally, it means act of faith. Its usage,
however, belongs to the Spanish Inquisition and a ritual-
istic act of faith required of so-called heretics; in that era
the expression also applied to the judgment against a
heretic, usually burning at the stake. Since the crucifixion
of Christ was also an attempt to do away with a dangerous
or heretical preacher, we can incorporate this meaning into
the general thought that natural life goes on while stu-
pendous things happen abroad. Given Emily Dickinson's
customary subjectifying of her verse, though, it would be
legitimate to bring the idea of "judgment against" down to
a personal level—to herself, perhaps, and her deprivation
of a fantasied love figure. In this sense the reference to
"Calvary" and the remarks about the bee would seem to
apply to the poet's feelings of loss. There are also sensual
overtones in the bee's separation from his rose, which of
course separates him from the possibility of honey. This
honey might be roughly equated with content, happiness,
for the poet.

The last stanza might be further interpreted this way. The

first two lines suggest tribunals sitting in awesome judgment, impressive speculations about meanings and interpretations of the Word—in other words, theorizing, intellectualizing, hair-splitting of the sort characteristic of Orthodox Churchdom. An idealized and somewhat unreal world is evoked in these first two lines, then, in sharp contrast to the "pragmatism" or solid practicality of the last two. The problems of the bee are simple, real, immediate, amounting to his needs and his deprivations or satisfactions. He knows what he knows because he experiences it instead of theorizing about it. This is a very credible reading of the last stanza, given Dickinson's constant concern with the immediacy of experience, her impatience with abstracts unless they are brought down to earth and earthly life.

TO MAKE A PRAIRIE IT TAKES A CLOVER AND ONE BEE

This is the charm and wit of Emily Dickinson, her capacity to chisel insight into absolute compactness (or, as the Greek poet Sappho, to whom Dickinson has been compared, once said, "polish clean as bone"). The wit is twinkling, yet wry, for the poem has also that air of one conscious of isolation from the world.

> To make a prairie it takes a clover and one bee,—
> And revery.
> The revery alone will do
> If bees are few.

Part of the instant impact of the poem stems from its virtual abandonment of form; the first line, for example, is uncommonly long. The length of the first line, however, prepares for the abrupt twist "and revery" of the second line: after all, one clover and one bee can hardly be said to make up a prairie. But here the poet is delightfully able to turn the wit upon herself, certainly the daydreamer, by remarking that revery—one's imagination—can do the job alone if necessary. There is a comment here about poetic method itself—that is, a sly pronouncement about its dependence upon the imagination.

IT DROPPED SO LOW IN MY REGARD

This little poem is one long series of delightfully sustained figures of speech, all created by Dickinson's conventional use of metaphors and similes drawn from familiar material of everyday life. Literally, the first stanza says that something or somebody has dropped very low in her regard. The second stanza, however, somewhat curiously blames "fate" more than her own self for the choice of friends, thus blaming fate rather than herself for this loss.

> **COMMENT:** Couched in folk idiom, the image of the first stanza is quite concrete; that is, before the reader comes to terms with the subtler meaning of "it," he is obliged to regard it as a stone or a piece of china. The latter turns out to be the case, since it goes "to pieces on the stones" at the bottom of the speaker's mind (mind is thus likened to the pavement below a high window, or even a well). The familiar phrases from everyday speech are of course to "drop low in somebody's regard," "I heard it hit the ground," "go to pieces," and in the second stanza, "reviled." Yet "fate," we are told, "fractured" this metaphoric china, and is to be blamed more than the speaker, who entertained "plated wares" on a shelf filled with silver.

> **RELIGIOUS OVERTONES.** Since the possibility of a rejected friend who fell below expectations has already been considered in the Introduction, let us turn to another interpretation of the "it." This possibility is Emily Dickinson's puzzlement and growing doubt and disillusionment about the traditional Calvinist religion in which she was brought up. Her family and neighbors identified essentially with the Trinitarian Congregationalists, then considered

the "Orthodox Church" as opposed to the "heretical" Unitarians, although through her life she declined to join this church. "It," meaning the traditional faith, can be read rather easily into the poem. These religious tenets dropped low in her regard, and here *mind* takes on more meaning, since it implies her reflections on ideology and the fact that this ideology fell to pieces at the *bottom* of her mind. *Fate* also becomes more meaningful in this interpretation, implying that some disenchantment with the rigid tenets of Calvinism was inevitable, and she did not "revile" herself—feel guilty about it—except for "entertaining plated wares/ Upon my silver shelf." Since "entertaining" is associated with entertaining an idea, loss of faith is a better interpretation here than loss of friends. Too much idealism, however, represented by the "silver," will cover either interpretation, just as "plated wares" may suggest an imperfect or flawed relationship—a cheaper relationship than the "silver" one—as well as a cheapened or impure ideal.

I DIED FOR BEAUTY, BUT WAS SCARCE

The literal content here can as usual be quickly stated. The first stanza relates the meeting in the tomb of one who died for beauty with one who died for truth. The second repeats this point, although it is referred to as "failure," and the man states that they are "brethren." The third stanza records their conversing together, as "kinsmen" who have come upon each other in the night, "until the moss had reached our lips,/ And covered up our names," or actually, until decay has set in and they are forgotten.

COMMENT: This is one of those poems which raises the question of Emily Dickinson's obsession with death. Although its subject matter seems to be a bit of philosophizing about beauty and truth (perhaps after the manner of the English poet Keats, whose poems were among the few she was acquainted with), the setting is the tomb. This setting is the source of a macabre, even somewhat distasteful quality in the poem, particularly in its ending, which conjures up the image of physical decay after death.

The poem must be examined in these twin lights, then, of subject matter and setting. To "die" for beauty or for truth, we assume, can mean actual death or can suggest a kind of poetic dedication to either. Probably Dickinson here means she was primarily devoted to the beautiful, which would include what she observed within her small sphere of the natural, the human and the supernatural. By truth—we simply cannot be sure from the context of the poem—she may be referring to philosophical or religious truth, or she may just mean, more generally, any abstract ideas. But the line, "The two are one," clearly hints at an influence by Keats, who was one of her favorite poets. In terms of subject matter, then, the last stanza records a secret and welcome communication with a fellow: "We talked between the rooms."

There is no escaping the fact, however, that the setting of the poem is an uncomfortable one, and with respect to the last stanza especially, comes near to spoiling the poem. When the reader allows himself to picture the situation, it becomes slightly grotesque; there is also a suggestive intimacy about it, in the spirit of the 17th century poet John Donne, whose poems of love and death have frequently been compared to Emily Dickinson's. Two barely dead bodies "scarce adjusted in the tomb" lie in adjoining graves (called "rooms," which strains quaintness into eccentricity) and chat about truth and beauty until they are devoured by the natural elements. It is a situation like, but more ludicrous than, that of those thwarted lovers of Greek mythology, Pyramus and Thisbe, who, separated by a restraining but real parental wall, conversed through a tiny hole.

Yet the point to be made about this poem's setting is somewhat pathetic: Emily Dickinson was irresistibly drawn to ideas of death and immortality, and her more and more morbid inclination to inject this note into all her poems shows her troubled spirit. It is not surprising, then, that both her best and her worst efforts hinge upon this theme. As Aiken remarks, "She seems to have thought of it constantly—she died all her life, she probed death daily." She herself wrote on another occasion that "bareheaded life under grass worries one like a wasp"—again displaying that capacity for homely metaphor ("bareheaded life," "worries one like a *wasp*") combined with awesome insight which is her forte.

INFLUENCE OF KEATS.   One of her biographers points out, with respect to the debt to Keats's "Ode on a Grecian Urn" in this poem: "It was characteristic of her passion for immediacy that she translated Keats's abstractions into terms of human figures. Nothing in Keats can quite match the eerie imagination of the last stanza, but in other respects the two poets have something in common."

THE HEART ASKS PLEASURE FIRST

This poem sounds almost like Emily Dickinson's version of the child's prayer, "Now I lay me down to sleep." It includes a rather prosaic list of requests that seem to be addressed, at least indirectly, to the Almighty: pleasure, excuse from pain, deadened suffering, to go to sleep, and, at length, to die.

> **COMMENT:**   It is not a good poem. First of all, the abundance of abstractions and clichés—heart, pleasure, pain, suffering, go to sleep—is not freshened by Dickinson's customary linguistic adventures, excepting perhaps *anodynes* and *Inquisitor*. It is not poeticized statement (as are the "Renunciation" or the "Remorse" poems) but

prose statement, which leads to a second objection: Contrary to her occasional "waywardness" of rhythm, the predominantly three-foot lines are unrelieved and sing-song. Even the structure of the sentences is monotonous, much too repetitive, a defect common to Emily Dickinson's poorer poems.

The heart asks pleasures first,
And then, excuse from pain;
And then, those little anodynes
That deaden suffering;

And then, to go to sleep;
And then, if it should be
The will of its Inquisitor,
The liberty to die.

The only intriguing element is the reference to God as the heart's (soul's, we presume) "Inquisitor," a rather harsh term reminiscent of one of the cruelest, bloodiest and bigoted periods of Christianity, the Spanish Inquisition. There is a hint, then—but an undeveloped hint—that the poet expects at death to face some sort of inquisition for her personal religious heresy during life. "Liberty to die" is the final, depressing note, indicating once more a pessimistic view of life. It is the concept of death-in-life again, the thought that life is hardly worth living. The truth is, though, that underneath it all Emily Dickinson seems to have considered that life was worth living, and commenting about. Perhaps this, the commentary, is the key. As Austin Warren rightly points out, "Reading her work does not induce despair. For herself first, and then for her readers, the very articulation of despair is effectual movement towards its dispelling." Her articulation of despair was her purgation, an idea as ancient as Greek tragedy and as modern as psychoanalysis.

IF I CAN STOP ONE HEART FROM BREAKING

This may be the worst poem Emily Dickinson ever wrote, unless there are still any unpublished poems. This, however, seems unlikely, after the flurry of editing and publishing that began in the twenties and culminated in Thomas H. Johnson's authoritative edition from the manuscripts acquired by Harvard in 1950. It is a masterpiece of cliché and sentimentality, and is included here to illustrate the tendency toward sentimentality, not only in Emily Dickinson's poetry, but in literature in general. It is, in other words, one of those occasions, fortunately not too frequent, where she has violated most of the principles of method we have praised her for. Making abstracts concrete; using quaint, inspired words and phrases; giving multiple levels of meaning (nature, impermanence and eternity converging in the same poem, for instance), an originality and fearlessness of thought, a spirit of adventure and stubborn waywardness of rhythm and rhyme, decided wit—all are here lacking. Almost every line contains a cliché:

> If I can stop one *heart from breaking,*
> I shall not *live in vain;*
> If I can *ease one life the aching,*
> Or cool one pain,
> Or help *one fainting robin*
> Unto his nest again,
> I *shall not live in vain.*

COMMENT: Worthy as such sentiments are—and the enactment of them worthier still (although one is thankful that she placed the fainting robin last in the hierarchy of those to be assisted)—the expression is entirely devoid of poetic value. The only possible response of any discerning reader (unless it be a horselaugh) is an uncomfortable sensation of whining and none-too-genuine piety.

A THOUGHT WENT UP MY MIND TODAY

All three stanzas of this poem elaborate on the idea of the return of a half-finished thought—a thought which remains unspecified. The poem seems to record that phenomenon of the consciousness whereby something does recur, presumably by association with some other random thing; and the seemingly accidental recurrence gives cause for wonderment.

COMMENT: The poet is talking to herself, and not very startlingly. The first line is the most distinguished in terms of language, since the figure of speech suggested is that of a chimney, a homely figure: the thought, like smoke (which is also somewhat ethereal and insubstantial went *up* the poet's mind, which is not the customary way of recording such things. Much of the remainder of the poem is prosaic, though—"I could not fix the year," for example, or "Nor definitely what it was," in the second stanza, or "It just reminded me—'twas all," in the third. In the second stanza, the smoke-thought metaphor is carried on in the idea that the thought seemed to have neither origin nor destination: "Nor where it went, nor why it came" (which seems to move, in fact, independently of the speaker), "Have I the art to say." The third stanza is most enigmatic of all, giving no hint as to what the thought (or indeed, feeling) was, being nearly as half-finished as the poet says the thought was:

But somewhere in my soul, I know
I've met the thing before;
It just reminded me—'twas all—
And came my way no more.

We might add, however, that in a modest way the theme of change and impermanence is asserted in this poem too, along with the lack of autonomy of the individual. Thoughts come and go, are molded in the consciousness, in some mysterious way; there are more half-answers than whole ones, the poet seems to be saying.

'TWAS SUCH A LITTLE, LITTLE BOAT

This is Emily Dickinson playing the "little girl," as she occasionally did (although sometimes with the simultaneous effect of flippant irony or sophisticated wit, as in the "I'm nobody" poem). Technically, it is child's poetry, except for the undertone of self-pity, even petulance, in the emerging thought that the world has neglected her.

'Twas such a little, little boat
That toddled down the bay!
'Twas such a gallant, gallant sea
That beckoned it away!

'Twas such a greedy, greedy wave
That licked it from the coast;
Nor ever guessed the stately sails
My little craft was lost!

COMMENT: The silliest elements are of course the coy repetitions: little, little boat; gallant, gallant sea; greedy, greedy wave. It is obvious that the "little boat" or "little craft" is the poet herself, obscure from the world, devoured by it, if we are to believe the terminology of the "greedy wave" and the "stately sails" which ignore her "little craft" until it is lost in the "gallant sea." Of course, in fairness to the thought of the poem (not to the technique) we must grant it a grain or two of pathos; it suggests that the girl who was Emily Dickinson first went forth into the world (of Amherst, and Boston, perhaps) much like any young person, filled with expectations of social success, some few happy and close human relationships, perhaps a more average later life of domesticity. Still, this is the poet with heart on sleeve, and one wishes from a critical point of view that such a poem had not seen print. (For a considerably more literarily acceptable version of the same theme—even the same figure of the boat—see the poem "It tossed and tossed.")

IT TOSSED AND TOSSED

The essence of this poem is the same as that of " 'Twas such a little, little boat," but the end product is somewhat improved. Literally, a "little brig" in the first stanza is "O took by blast," and gropes toward the morning. The second stanza reveals, though, that the "brig" slipped and slipped and finally "dropped from sight," capsized. The third stanza is an "epitaph" for the brig, for which the "ocean's heart" is "too smooth, too blue" to make way.

> COMMENT: The little brig, like the "little boat," is somebody's life, perhaps the poet's, tossing none too originally on the sea of life. As contrasted to the "little boat" poem, however, the repetitions work for it, producing an image of the spinning "drunken" little brig and the tossing sea. The language is altogether tighter; most especially, the sentimentality and self-pity of the other poem are here absent. The story is made much less personal by the poet's statement, "A little brig *I knew*." And the poem manages to operate successfully on two levels, the literal one of a real boat on a real sea, and the metaphoric one of a life caught in the "blast" or storms of life. This makes the last two lines of the first stanza, for instance, more effective: "It spun and spun/ And groped delirious, for morn." *Delirious* is a useful term, suggestive of the appearance of a boat in a storm or of a person fevered. The second stanza is somewhat awkward in rhythm and rhymes:

It slipped and slipped,
As one that drunken stepped;
Its white foot tripped,
Then dropped from sight.

LANGUAGE. While the metaphor of the drunken person unites nicely with *delirious* in the first stanza, and "white foot" can mean the prow of the boat or an actual human foot, *slipped, stepped, tripped* do not make for harmonious sound effects; and the line "then dropped from sight" is not only prosaic but needs another "foot" of meter (two beats) to balance the second line of this stanza. The last stanza's touching thought is that the "ocean's heart," i.e., the world's heart, is too inflexible to make way for the brig ("to break for you"). But the simple repetition of *you* in lines two and four is needless, and one wonders why the poet did not make the tiny improving revision of interchanging *crew* and *you* in line two:

Ah, brig, good-night
To *you* and *crew;*
The ocean's heart too smooth, too blue,
To break for you.

FOR EACH ECSTATIC INSTANT

Even in recording joy, this poet cannot get rid of the idea of pain and the Calvanist principle of payment, especially for pleasure, which is distrusted. This distrust seems to have been absorbed into Emily Dickinson's consciousness. The first stanza is superior to the second, which is slightly redundant, although interesting.

For each ecstatic instant
We must an anguish pay
In keen and quivering ratio
To the ecstasy.

For each beloved hour
Sharp pittances of years,
Bitter contested farthings
And coffers heaped with tears.

COMMENT. In effect the principle proclaimed here is clear and harsh: an anguish, a pain is to be paid "in keen and quivering ratio." This is a vivid line in its suggestion, with *quivering* especially, of the piercing shaft of an arrow. This is one of her perfectly neat and compact stanzas. "For each beloved hour" is a little bland and flat, somewhat redeemed by "sharp pittances of years" (although the use of *pittances*—meager sums—seems a little dubious and inappropriate to the grand scale of "ecstasy" suggested). The cumulative effect of the last three lines of the second stanza is good, though, since "pittances of years," "bitter contested farthings," and "coffers heaped with tears" amass, figuratively, a huge payment for those "ecstatic instants."

MUCH MADNESS IS DIVINEST SENSE

This semi-serious poem makes a pronouncement of the relationship between the individual and society, asserting in the first three lines that "much madness" may seem "divinest sense/ To a discerning eye," whereas "much sense" may be "starkest madness." It is the angle of vision that counts, and the poet believes that " 'Tis the majority/ In this, as all, prevails." If you "assent" —conform—you are accepted, or "sane"; if you "demur" you are considered dangerous and handled like an insane person or an animal.

COMMENT: This flippant, somewhat tongue-in-cheek observation on the individual's relation to the rest of the world—especially the slightly eccentric individual—compares in ironic wit to the more popular

I'm nobody! Who are you?
Are you nobody, too?
Then there's a pair of us—don't tell!
They'd banish us, you know.

How dreary to be somebody!
How public, like a frog
To tell your name the livelong day
To an admiring bog!

In either case, the poet seems to be defending her own
position and isolated way of life. While the "I'm nobody"
poem is little-girl-like, it manages to avoid being childishly
simple (like the "little, little boat" poem) through dry wit.
"Much madness . . ." is even more sophisticated and wit-
tily ironic, as well as more enriched by linguistic combinations and more scornful toward society and its systems of
conformity. The first three lines are vivid but need hardly
be explicated since they speak for themselves. Notice the
inclusion of one of her favorite words, *divine*. "Starkest
madness," used to characterize sense that passes for sense
but isn't (pedantry, perhaps; overintellectualization; pious
hypocrisy), is effective in its vague association with "na-
kedness." This association indicates that those very people
who feel themselves safely clothed in sensible thought or
philosophy may be, from a mental point of view, running
about naked. The complaint of the poet is frankly voiced
in the remaining lines: there is no escaping it, the majority
prevails in everything. There is no room for individuality,
as evidenced by the blunt closing lines: "Demur,—you're
straightway dangerous,/ And handled with a chain." There
is some question whether "handled with a chain" is a vul-
garizing touch to an otherwise sophisticated piece. In any
case the point is abruptly got across, perhaps with an in-
direct reference to the inhumane and often brutal manner
in which the mentally ill were handled until very recent
times.

I FELT A FUNERAL IN MY BRAIN

This is a five-stanza poem on the nature of mental anguish. The
poet conveys a sense of the mental pain which is torturing her

by speaking of the pain as if it were a funeral being carried on in her mind. In stanza one, the poet states that she "felt a funeral" in her mind. She focuses particularly on the heavy and constant tread of the mourners' feet, and says that it seemed as though the sense world were breaking into the world ordinarily reserved for the mind. In stanza two, the poet continues the figure of the funeral. Now, with the mourners seated and the service beginning, a drumming noise associated with the service numbs her mind. In stanza three, the poet states that she hears the mourners lift the coffin. Again, they move slowly across her soul with feet which seem encased in lead. In stanza four, the figure is continued in the sound of a tolling bell. The heaven seems to have become a great bell which is ringing, and all creation responds as though it were an ear. In the last two lines, she introduces the image of a shipwreck. The poet personifies silence, and says that it seemed as though she and silence had been stranded together, thus constituting an unusual race. In stanza five, the poet compares reason to a plank of wood which breaks as a result of being overstrained. The image is continued with the poet dropping away from this broken plank into a universe filled with new worlds.

COMMENT: The poem is an interesting and extremely complex statement on the relationship between the body and the soul during a time of mental anguish. The imagery of stanza evokes the mind in a state of mental shock. The mourners' feet symbolize the entire sense world, which is pressing on the poet's consciousness and threatening to throw it into a state of complete disorder. In stanza two, the image of the seated mourners suggests that some order has been restored. However, the mind is again under attack, and the beating drum symbolizes the waves of feeling which numb the mind. In stanza three, the poet suggests an intensification of the attack on the mind by bringing together images of sound and weight. She hears the mourners as they lift the coffin and begin to move, and she feels their feet which seem to be encased in lead. In stanza four, the poet shifts to a new image, that of a shipwreck, which increases the feeling of desolation which the mind experiences. The attack of the sense world reaches a climax in this stanza as the world is filled with the sound of ringing bells. Finally, the image in the last stanza suggests that the mental anguish has become too much, and that the sense world has won out and a complete mental breakdown has occurred. The image is that of the speaker falling through infinite space. It suggests that the order which the mind imposes on reality has been disrupted, that the speaker is no longer subject to the mind.

I HEARD A BUZZ WHEN I DIED

Dickinson's preoccupation with death is once again revealed in this four-stanza poem. In stanza one, the speaker sets the scene. She is on her death bed, and her tone is more that of the dispassionate observer than that of the dying individual. She evokes the atmosphere of death by focusing on the silence in the room and on the buzzing sound of a fly. In stanza two, the speaker turns her attention to those who are witnessing her death. Their eyes are dry from prolonged crying, and they are preparing themselves to face the actual fact of death. In stanza three, the speaker turns back to herself and the making of her will. She imagines herself signing over to her heirs everything but her body and soul. It is then that a fly attracts her attention. In stanza four, the speaker evokes the actual moment of death by focusing on the fly. She notes the blueness of the fly, its intermittent buzzing, and finally the way in which the fly seems to blot out all of the light in the room.

COMMENT: The poem presents an acute analysis of the psychology of death. It concerns itself with the wedge which death drives between the senses and the spirit, and the final obliteration of the spirit itself. In the first three stanzas, the speaker becomes progressively dissociated from the sense world. The fly of the first stanza suggests that the body has already begun to decay. By focusing on the silence broken only by the buzzing of the fly, the speaker suggests that her other senses no longer respond to the world, that she has been cut off from the sense world. The feeling of being separated from the sense world is intensified in stanza two by the dispassionate way in which the dying speaker observes the people attending her death. She no longer operates through her senses or through her feelings; she has been reduced to pure intellect by the approach of death. In stanza three a further separation between the individual and the sense world is suggested through the signing of the will. The speaker first psychologically and then legally is cut off from the world of things. Finally, the complete failure of the senses and of the consciousness is suggested in stanza four. The poet powerfully conveys the shrinking of human consciousness by allowing a fly to become a measure of that consciousness. For a person in full possessions of his powers, a fly is no more than a minor irritation. Its sound, size, and color are for the most part simply ignored. However, here, the sound and size of the fly can completely overpower the weakened senses of the speaker.

THE FIRST DAY'S NIGHT HAD COME

This five-stanza poem deals with the psychological effects of shock. In stanza one, the speaker conveys her emotional state at the end of a day which has begun with an extremely shocking experience. She expresses her relief at having been able to get through the day, and she tells her soul that it should rejoice. In stanza two, the soul's reply is given. The soul says that it has been broken apart and that it needs time to restore itself. The image used is that of a bow which has been shattered. Stanza three deals with the speaker's emotional state on the following day. Instead of the shock being lessened on the second day, it becomes more intense. The experience is twice as difficult to face, and the horror of the experience is once again felt,

Instead of the shock being lessened on the second day, it becomes more intense. The experience is twice as difficult to face, and the horror of the event is once again felt. In stanzas four and five, the speaker focuses on the prolonged effects of the horrible experience. The speaker's brain is personified as a madman. It is driven mad by the experience and begins to laugh. As the years pass, the brain continues its foolish laughing. The speaker contemplates her changed situation and wonders if this is what the world calls madness.

> **COMMENT:**   The poet avoids sensationalism and sentimentality by refusing to reveal the nature of the shocking experience. By not specifying, she also universalizes the experience. The poem gains intensity as a result of the ironic turn in stanza three. The dialogue between the self and the soul which occurs in the first two stanzas implies that time will lessen the shock and heal the psychological wound that's been inflicted. Ironically, however, the reverse is true. In stanza three, with the dawn of a new day, the horror of the experience is doubled, not lessened. In the last two stanzas, not only is the wound not healed, but it becomes permanent. A large part of the poem's power derives from the ironic contrast between the dispassionate voice of the speaker and the emotion-charged content.

THE LAST NIGHT THAT SHE LIVED

This seven-stanza poem deals with the death of a friend, and the way in which that death affects the speaker's relationship with the world. In stanza one, the speaker says that only the fact of the friend's death made this particular night different from any other. In stanza two, the speaker says that the death affected her relationship with nature. She began to notice things that she had previously overlooked. In stanzas three and four, the speaker turns her attention to the other people present. Her relationship to them has also changed. The fact that they are living and that they will continue to live makes the speaker intensely aware of the friend's imminent death. She puts herself in the dying friend's place and becomes jealous of the life which these others have. In stanza five, the speaker says that the souls of those present were too upset for them to be able to communicate among themselves. In stanza six, the death itself is described. The speaker compares the friend to a reed which wavers and then at the moment of death bends towards the water. In stanza seven, the speaker describes the way in which the body is disposed after death, and then speaks of the "awful leisure" which is suddenly theirs as a result of the death.

> **COMMENT:**   The climactic phrase in the poem is the "awful leisure" of the last stanza. It is ironic that leisure should be thought of as awful, but it is precisely this irony which is at the heart of the poem. In the first six stanzas, the speaker is wholly engaged in the event of death. There is a great deal of physical, mental, and emotional activity. The speaker notices things ordinarily overlooked; she walks from room to room; she feels things about other people that she wouldn't ordinarily feel; she arranges the corpse after death. This activity is the antithesis of leisure. One would, in a normal situation, be relieved to gain leisure time after such intense activity. However, the leisure gained by death is awful since for the first time the speaker will be open to the full effect of death.

'TWAS LIKE A MAELSTROM, WITH A NOTCH

This six-stanza poem deals with the anxiety caused by uncertainty, probably in regard to love. In the first stanza, the poet compares this uncertainty to a whirlpool which comes closer each day. Stanza two deals with the agony of suspense. Agony toys with the hem of her dress, and then suddenly she feels herself falling as if in a dream. Stanza three introduces a nightmare creature who watches the time carefully, looking forward to the moment when it will have captured the speaker. In the last two lines of the stanza the speaker feels herself caught between the creature's paws. Stanza four elaborates upon her situation. She is completely helpless in the creature's grasp when God remembers and forces it to release her. Stanza five concerns the certainty of despair. If her hopes were to be dashed once and for all, she would be like the prisoner who had received his sentence, only to be led from her cell to the hangman. Stanza six considers the possibility of a last-minute reprieve, and once again the speaker's uncertainty is restored. Finally, in the last two lines the speaker wonders which state would result in the greater pain, the state of uncertainty or the certainty of despair.

> **COMMENT:** Dickinson evokes the anguish caused by uncertainty through a succession of nightmarish images. There is the image of the whirlpool, coming ever closer; there is the image of the goblin lying in wait for her; there is the image in which she has been caught between the creature's paws; there is the image of a God who can carelessly forget about the speaker and her predicament. The poem has psychological complexity in that the speaker enjoys the agony of doubt.

WILD NIGHTS—WILD NIGHTS

This is a three-stanza love poem. In stanza one, the speaker addresses the object of her love, and says that were they together the nights would be exciting, pleasure-filled. In stanza two, the speaker introduces the image of a ship at port. She compares herself to this ship, which no longer has use for charts or compasses. Finally, in stanza three, the speaker expresses a desire to be with the object of her love. She again compares herself to a boat and the object of her love to the sea in which she would moor.

> **COMMENT:** The ecstasy of love is evoked through the sailing images. By comparing herself to a sailboat before the wind, she suggests the buoyancy, lightheartedness, and yet strength and durability of love. In stanza two, the

image of the boat in port suggests the safety of her present situation, and yet also the lifelessness of this situation. The woman separated from the object of love is like the sailboat away from the wind and the sea; it no longer realizes itself. Finally, by comparing the object of her love to the sea, she suggests the scope of her feeling. It, like the sea, is infinite.

A BIRD CAME DOWN THE WALK

This is a five-stanza study of a bird in motion. In stanza one, the speaker watches as a bird finds an angleworm and bites it in two. In stanza two, the bird drinks the dew from the grass and steps aside for a beetle. In stanza three, the speaker draws attention to the bird's frightened eyes, which she compares to beads. In stanza four, the speaker offers the cautious bird a crumb, but instead of accepting the gift it flies away. The motion of the bird's wings is compared to the motion of a boat's oars. In the final stanza, the speaker continues the comparison of the bird's wings to oars, but says that the sound of the flying bird is softer than the sound of oars cutting through the water, and softer in fact than the sound of butterflies swimming through the noonday air.

COMMENT: Dickinson demonstrates her ability to see two aspects of reality at the same time, its ugliness and its beauty. Beetles and angleworms are not ordinarily subjects which lend themselves to poetic treatment. Yet she takes nature at its ugliest and most primitive, and transforms it through her humor and imaginative approach. She could have approached the bird's capture of the angleworm as an object lesson in the survival of the fittest; instead, she treats the bird as though it were simply someone with bad manners. The bird's beauty is conveyed through the emphasis she gives to its "velvet head" and its graceful and soundless motion. She captures the essence of the bird's movement by carefully attending to its frenetic actions. In quick succession the bird bites the angleworm in half, drinks the dew, hops sideways, glances from side to side wary of danger, and then flies away.

I DWELL IN POSSIBILITY

This poem is one of Dickinson's statements about the importance of imagination and the limitations of reason. She begins by stating that she lives within "possibility"; she is a creature of the imagined rather than of "Prose," the limited here-and-now. This house of imagination is superior to the house of fact; there are more outlets onto the world, more doors and windows. The second stanza compares the house of imagination to a great cedar forest which cannot be penetrated by an unfriendly eye, and which has as its roof the limitless reaches of the sky. In the last stanza, the poet describes her "visitors" in the house of imagination (her thoughts and fancies) as "the fairest" or best guests that she could have. Her final statement is that, in the Imagination, she need only stretch her limited, human hands, to be in contact with Paradise itself.

> **COMMENT:** This poem is an excellent example of the poet's magnificent power of compression, her ability to pare down her poetry to give the most possible meaning in the fewest possible words. The reader must supply a good part of the sentence, but the meaning is never really obscured. For example, the line "Of chambers, as the cedars—" must be read as an extension of the first stanza. Thus, one reads "I dwell in a house with chambers" which, like "the cedars," are "Impregnable of eye" (cannot be penetrated by the eye of an outsider). The second sentence of this stanza also requires additions by the reader; when these additions are made, it reads: "And for an everlasting roof" there are "The gables of the sky." Gables here refer to the extensions which used to be built on the roofs of houses.

This one stanza gives examples of the two techniques which are most often required to read Dickinson's compressed, elliptical poetry. In the first line the necessary material can be found by referring to the previous stanza (the key words, "I dwell" and "house," can be found there). In the second line he can refer to his own common sense, since the practice of leaving out an "understood" verb is a common one. The reason why Dickinson's poetry is more difficult than some is that she leaves out so very many words. In this poem, for example, every verb but the first ("dwell") must be supplied by the reader.

I TASTE A LIQUOR NEVER BREWED

This poem is a symbolic statement on the source of poetic inspiration and the nature of poetic thought. The poet begins by saying that she tastes a liquor; she is becoming intoxicated. She immediately states that this is no ordinary drink; it does not come from cups of valuable material or valuable workmanship ("tankards scooped in pearl"), nor is it any particular kind of brew (beer, the product of "vats upon the Rhine"). The second stanza states the source of her intoxication. She is drunk on the simplest things of a summer day: air, dew, the sky ("inns of molten blue"). She continues the imagery of a New England summer in the third stanza, stating that after the bees and butterflies had drunk their fill of the flowers' nectar, she would still not be satisfied. The last stanza is a gently irreverent statement that she, the simple, nature-loving poet, will turn the heavens on end; she will drink the intoxicating liquor of the flowers till saints run to the windows of heaven and the mightiest of angels lift their hats to her. The last two lines are particularly significant, since they state that the poet who is intoxicated on flowers and dew can transcend space; the "little tippler," the poet, is "leaning against the sun." She is truly inspired.

COMMENT: This poem, much like "I dwell in possibility," is a statement on the source of true inspiration, and, by extension, a comment on the kind of material which produces real poetry. The poet's liquor is none of the traditional ones, nor does it come from a cup. It comes from the out-of-doors, and this liquor must be consumed to the point of intoxication. Only when intoxicated can the poet lean against the sun; thus, only when the poet forsakes reason for intuition can he see the truth of the world. The ideas in both poems are much like the ideas of the English and American romantic poets. The poet must turn to nature to discover what is valuable. He must trust his emotions, not his head; he must, in fact, attempt to transcend even his own emotions, to produce true poetry. Ralph Waldo Emerson and Edgar Allan Poe, famous American poets who wrote immediately before Emily Dickinson, wrote similar hymns to emotional intoxication in "Merlin" and "Israfel," respectively.

HOPE IS THE THING WITH FEATHERS

This is a deceptively simple poem, which though short and apparently very clear, is really quite complex. The whole poem is built around the image of hope as a "thing with feathers," in other words, a bird of some kind. Hope is figured as a bird who dwells in the soul, singing a wordless but inspiring song which never stops. This song can be heard during whatever storm and stress may assail an individual; nothing can "abash" (quell or quiet) it, and it lives everywhere, on the farthest land and in the most hostile seas. The most remarkable thing about this bird, the poet concludes, is its generosity. While providing a song of consolation and comfort in all kinds of distress, it never asks anything in return from the person whose soul is its home.

COMMENT: This entire poem is one metaphor; it is a description of the quality "hope," in which every characteristic of that abstraction is told in the concrete terms of a bird and its song. Thus, hope lives in the soul; it is wordless, and so it appeals to the heart rather than to the mind. It continues its comfort through the harshest of circumstances, and in the unfriendliest of environments; finally, it is completely unselfish. These qualities of hope, if listed as abstractions, might make a fine sermon or philosophical essay; because Dickinson has concretized them, however, has described a warm, comforting, happy bird in terms of the qualities which hope possesses, she has created a vivid and memorable picture rather than an abstract description.

I LIKE TO SEE IT LAP THE MILES

This poem is an extended description and personification of a railroad train. By ascribing to a train the qualities of an animate being (personification) the poet gives a graphic and vivid description of it. The poet pictures the train just as a child might; it seems to be some kind of gigantic animal which can lap up miles and lick off valleys as if they were nothing. The "prodigious" (gigantic) train eats at tanks, steps around mountains, peers haughtily into the insignificant houses by its roadbed, slithers through a rock quarry, all the while hurrying itself to its own stable door—the depot where it stops.

> COMMENT: While the poem uses a childish view and at times childlike terminology ("horrid, hooting stanza," "chase itself down the hill"), there is nothing childish about its structure. The entire statement is made by indirection. That is, the poet never tells the reader that she is describing a train; rather, she gives a description so accurate and imaginative that the reader sees the train for himself. The metaphor which is used throughout the poem is that of some kind of huge, snorting animal which rushes over the land, complaining and shouting, then stops at its own door. In this technique the poet captures at once the behavior of a train, which certainly does rush headlong over the land, taking mountains and valleys in its stride and shrieking as it goes; and at the same time she captures

the significance of this behavior. The only difference between the train and a monster is that the train is under the control of something rational. It does not go on a rampage forever, but stops where it belongs. Two words in the last stanza, "docile" and "omnipotent," are particularly significant. The train, a huge piece of machinery, ought to be omnipotent or all-powerful. It is not, however; it is docile, or obedient, because despite its physical power it is controlled by the mind of man. This is why it is "punctual as a star"; this is why it always stops where it should.

A NARROW FELLOW IN THE GRASS

This poem is a good example of Dickinson's treatment of nature. Here she describes a snake, and the description is obviously prompted by accurate knowledge of her subject. She ends the poem, however, not with the snake itself, but with an acknowledgement of the feeling of apprehension which he inspires. Throughout the poem the snake is never named; he simply remains "a narrow fellow," riding in the grass and appearing without warning. The further descriptions make it clear, however, that it is a snake which is being described. The poet calls him a "spotted shaft," an unbraided whiplash opening and closing the grass as soundlessly as a comb would do. She goes on to describe the kind of habitat the snake likes; when a child, she found him in cool, boggy ground, where corn could not grow. The last two stanzas push the meaning of the poem further than description. The poet states that she feels positively delighted when she meets most of the animals she knows; she never sees the snake, however, whether alone or with others, without feeling a chill in the marrow of her bone and a tightening of her chest.

> COMMENT: In this poem the poet simply describes and acknowledges a situation, without giving any indication of why it should be so. The situation is the fear which she, and most other people, feels when she sees a snake.

This fear is a common one, and much has been written about it; Dickinson's description of it, however, is particularly powerful because of her technique. She does not simply state that she is frightened of snakes and that many other people are too; she spends the first four stanzas of the poem describing the snake as one might any other animal of which he was fond. The very phrase "narrow fellow" is a friendly sort of name. The fifth stanza also makes the shock of the last more powerful; the poet is not unacquainted with nature, not afraid of snakes because she hasn't seen many animals in her life. She is, in fact, on good terms with most of "nature's people"—they know her and she them. It is this preparation—a guileless description by a confirmed nature-lover—which makes the last stanza so effective. This fear of snakes is not a rational thing, the poet says; there is simply a feeling of menace connected with snakes which goes beyond reason and knowledge. Why this should be so, the poet does not say; she simply makes her observation.

PRESENTIMENT IS THAT LONG SHADOW ON THE LAWN

This poem, only four lines or 25 words long, is an excellent example of Dickinson's ability to communicate with an absolute minimum of words. The dictionary defines *presentiment* as: "a feeling or impression that something is about to happen, especially something evil; a foreboding." Dickinson also gives a definition in the poem; she begins "Presentiment is," but the entire definition is given as a metaphor. She compares presentiment, the feeling that something is about to happen, with a long shadow on the grass, a shadow which is a sign that night is approaching.

> **COMMENT:**   The poem can be paraphrased in a sentence or two, but it must be examined closely in order to detect the excellence and vividness of the definition. This poem exemplifies Dickinson's excellent vocabulary of

everyday words. She uses no exotic vocabulary here, but rather uses ordinary language with the greatest precision. Her use of the plural "suns" in the second line, for example lifts the meaning of the poem from specific to general; the shadow indicates, not one oncoming night, but many. Suns come up and sun will go down; thus, it is a general phenomenon that she describes. The first two lines take care of one part of the definition: presentiment is a feeling that something is going to happen, here a feeling that night is about to fall. Her use of the words "startled" and "darkness" in the last two lines takes care of the second part of the definition, that presentiment is a feeling of foreboding. The grass is startled, surprised, by the herald of night; and night itself is referred to as darkness. The grass seems unwilling to surrender itself to night; it has a feeling, a foreboding, that all may not be well in the dark. This poem indicates another quality of Dickinson's, her ability to communicate the feeling which a word conveys, rather than just a factual definition.

THE SKY IS LOW, THE CLOUDS ARE MEAN

In this two-stanza poem Dickinson writes of nature, one of her favorite subjects, but here it is nature at her worst. She paints the picture of the moments before a storm: the clouds are lowering and surly-looking, one snowflake drifts across the landscape. The wind, in the second stanza, is complaining and whining with self-pity. Nature, the poet concludes, is like all of us sometimes caught in a bad mood.

> **COMMENT:** This poem is illustrative of a nature poet who treats her subject honestly, painting the bad side as well as the good. The clouds and the wind are personified, given the qualities of human beings; they are "mean" and "complaining." The poet then compares nature without her jewels (her diadem) to human beings; each of us is sometimes mean or ugly. The meter of the poem is more

regular than many of Dickinson's; the pattern is a traditional ballad stanza. A four-beat line is followed by a three-beat line, and the rhyme scheme of the four-line stanzas is a b c d.

SAFE IN THEIR ALABASTER CHAMBERS

This poem, one of Dickinson's best-known works, contrasts the qualities of stillness with those of life. In the first stanza she emphasizes the timelessness of death; the "meek members of the resurrection" sleep in their coffins untouched by dawn or noon. They are sealed in, closed off from time and the world, by the oppressive weight of rafter and roof. The second stanza lists some of the joys of a summer day: the breeze laughs, the bees buzz, the birds sing. Their unknown wisdom is for nothing, however, since no one hears them. In the third stanza the poet goes from the movement of natural things to the movements of time; the years proceed in their orderly fashion, planets make their own prescribed orbits, and earthly kings rise and fall—but again, the dead are unaware of all this activity.

COMMENT: This poem is on one hand a statement on the awful unknowingness of death, the complete removal of the dead from all activity, the largest and the smallest. The dead are "safe" in their "alabaster chambers," but they are also completely removed from everything that a human being considers interesting or valuable. The poem can also be read as a statement on organized religion; the "meek members of the resurrection," those who have been "saved" by religion, are sealed from the world as effectively as if they were dead. In this sense it is, like many of Dickinson's poems, very similar to Transcendentalist thought. Churchgoers who worship under rafters and roof simply cut themselves off from the breezes and birds, the natural creatures who have true "sagacity" or wisdom.

The two readings do not contradict each other, however;

rather the poet seems to be saying that people who are blinded by a narrow religion suffer twice. They cannot be aware of the realities of the world when they are alive, for they will not let themselves see what is really happening; and when they are dead, they will never have the chance to make up for their mistake.

A CRITICAL SUMMARY

THEMES. Although Emily Dickinson wrote more than 1,500 poems in her life, she was remarkably consistent in the subjects which she chose to write about, as well as in the treatment which she gave those subjects. A look at her poetry will reveal that she most often wrote about death, love, mental pain, religion (her own and the traditional organized religions of her day), solitude, and nature. At times she was serious about those subjects, at times ironic or humorous; always, however, she dealt somehow with these preoccupations.

DEATH. Probably the subject which most fascinated Dickinson was death. Many of her most famous poems, including "I heard a fly buzz when I died," "Safe in their alabaster chambers," and others deal, with this theme. She often placed herself in the position of the person who was dying, in an attempt to convey some idea of what death must be like. At other times, for example in "The last night that she lived," she presents herself as one of the mourners who must watch a loved one dying and take care of the body after death. "Safe in their alabaster chambers" deals with death itself, rather than the death of an individual; here she contrasts the light and motion of life with the dark, timeless quality which is death.

IMMORTALITY. It is important to note that in none of the poems dealing with death does Dickinson indicate that she has any real faith in an afterlife. On the contrary, she concentrates on the complete removal of the dead, both physically and spiritually. Death, to Dickinson, is the absolute cessation of motion; apparently, she felt that death was indeed the end of everything.

LOVE. The subject of love, oddly enough, is closely connected to the subject of death in Dickinson's poetry. This is true because the love seen in her works is almost always unrequited love; that is, it is a love which is unknown to or not returned by the lover. Dickinson's love poetry generally portrays a longing for a passion she cannot have, or else her painful reaction to a love which she has had, but which has somehow been taken away from her. At its best, Dickinson's love poetry can be an astringent and dignified commentary on the pain of unreturned or impossible love; at its worst, it sometimes degenerates into self-pity or querulousness. "Wild nights! Wild nights!" is an example of her better love poetry; it is a description of love as being simply an involvement with life and one individual. " 'Twas like a maelstrom, with a notch," another excellent poem, considers a quite different aspect of the subject; it deals with the psychological torment connected with an uncertain love.

MENTAL PAIN. Another favorite theme of Dickinson's, closely connected with her investigations of love, is that of mental anguish. Such poems as "I felt a funeral in my brain," and "The first day's night had come" deal insistently and unsentimentally with the process of approaching madness or the possibility of madness. In her poems about mental pain Dickinson has proven herself to be an acute and observant psychologist; many of the phenomena which she described could constitute the case history of a real mental breakdown. Her psychological poems also point up another consistent characteristic of Dickinson's, that is, her refusal to accept the comfortable clichés which ordinary people often resort to. "The first day's night had come," for example, turns upside down the cliché that "things will be better tomorrow." In this poem of madness the first day is the best, since the mind is numbed by shock; it is in the second and succeeding days that the soul cannot bear its burden and the mind breaks apart.

TRADITIONAL RELIGION. Dickinson was not kind to the traditional ideas of God and religion in her poetry. "Renunciation is a piercing virtue," for example, gives a negative, narrow idea of religion which tries to make a positive virtue out of renunciation and deprivation and neglects the positive aspects of life. " 'Twas like a maelstrom, with a notch" describes God as a rather cynical, uninterested individual who suddenly remembers the poet's desperate plight only after she has suffered unnecessary torment. "I asked no other thing" gives the same idea of the "mighty maker," who is here compared to a haggling shopkeeper. This criticism of religion was always indirectly and subtly done, however, and a good deal of Dickinson's poetry bears testimony to an earnest and often unhappy attempt to reconcile herself with the religion of her childhood.

TRANSCENDENTALISM. The religious beliefs which were closest to Dickinson, however, were those of Transcendentalism. This movement emphasized an intuitive, emotional religion, rather than a rational one; it glorified the positive aspects of life (love of fellow man and love of God's creatures) rather than the negative. Transcendentalists also held that the outdoors was the place to find God, rather than the inside of a church where the worshippers were walled off by wood and stone. Much of Dickinson's poetry reflects these beliefs. In "I taste a liquor never brewed" she says that she, the poet drunk on the nectar of flowers, can soar higher than saints and angels. In "I never saw a moor" she makes a statement of faith; she can deduce God's existence because she has seen the beauties of his creation.

SOLITUDE. It is not surprising that Dickinson, who spent much of her life inside her own yard and even in her own house, should write many poems on the excellence of solitude and the danger of too much conformity. In "I dwell in Possibility" she implies that the proper place for a poet is a quiet spot where foreign eyes cannot penetrate. In "Much madness is divinest sense" she states that cold, rational knowledge is really madness, and charges that the world in general too often treats the nonconformist as if he were a madman, to be "handled with a chain."

NATURE. Another major category of Dickinson's poetry deals with birds and animals. In this nature poetry Dickinson is always objective; she describes the ugly details of nature as well as the beautiful ones. "A bird came down the walk" exemplifies this quality of her poetry; it also exemplifies another, her keenly observant eye. In this poem she manages to capture the essential qualities of the bird she describes, his quick, sharp movements, his beady eyes. The same thing is true of "A narrow fellow in the grass," where she gives a vivid picture not only of the appearance and habitat of the snake, but also of the feeling which he inspires in those who see him.

CRITICAL COMMENTARY

A SKETCH OF TRENDS IN CRITICISM TO THE PRESENT.   It is not unusual for literary figures to be largely ignored in their lifetimes; there are many examples from American literature, such as Nathaniel Hawthorne, Henry David Thoreau, Edgar Allan Poe, Herman Melville, and Henry James. It was quite natural for Emily Dickinson to miss recognition, however, because less than a dozen of her poems were published during her lifetime. Nobody, except a few friends and relatives, usually recipients of her correspondence, and one literary figure, Colonel Thomas Wentworth Higginson, knew about her verse until after her death. It was then that Wentworth and a family friend, Mabel Loomis Todd, put together the first small volume of poems. It is from this point, in 1890, that we measure the reception of Emily Dickinson's poetry.

MIXED REACTION.   The first decade of criticism of that poetry—1890-1900—probably illustrated the mixed reaction of her first literary friend and critic, Higginson, who had called her "wayward" and her meters "spasmodic"; that is, there were puzzlement and some outrage about the unorthodoxy of her poetry. For critics trained as academicians and scholars it was difficult to penetrate her unorthodox form and technique—indeed, her ignorance of such matters—to discover the originality of her thought and language. The early responses were varied, from the realization of the eminent William Dean Howells that she was a genius, if an eccentric one, to the patent dismissal by a British critic, Andrew Lang, of her work as ignorant and incompetent.

INCREASED RECOGNITION.   As more and more of her letters and poems were published, there was an increased awareness that she could not be ignored as a poet, an awareness which perhaps culminated in the 1920's, when the multiple, complicated aspects of her poetry and her personality—which we have since seen are inextricably woven together—received more attention. Critics began to discuss many elements: her unconventional form, problems of biography, her dominant themes, and questions of reliable texts. Critics moved away—and it was a most fortunate and just move—from their preconditioned ideals of poetry to a consideration of what Emily Dickinson's poetry was. In this period she was considered both "modern" and old-fashioned, for some linked her to another past age of "eccentric" poetry, the 17th century with its so-called "metaphysical poets" such as John Donne and George Herbert. It is known that she was well read in the writings of another literary figure of that earlier period, the mystic Henry Vaughan.

THE MODERN CRITICS.   From the period of the twenties and thirties to the present, there has been a growing and sensible assumption that her poetry is, in part at least, original and great. Critics have proceeded from that point in the spirit of the "new criticism," the method of precise explication and analysis of her poems, to discover what effects she has achieved linguistically, philosophically, and metaphysically. The modern critic's object is no longer to question her greatness, but to clarify it.

EARLY CRITICISM: 1890-1900.   Thomas Wentworth Higginson, valuable as he is as the sole literary figure among Emily Dickinson's correspondents, has generally been regarded as a somewhat timid, or at least puzzled, critic (in print) of her poetry; nevertheless, his comments are usefully representative of the period and its reaction to this poetry. He characterizes it in justice as the "life-work of a woman so secluded that she lived literally indoors by choice for many years, and within the limits of her father's estate for many more—who shrank even from the tranquil society of a New England college town, and yet loved her few friends with profound devotedness, and divided her life between them and her flowers." Thus, he observes, it "startles one" to find her intense visions of life and death. For he soon detected her preoccupation with the theme of death, time, and immortality, which produced some of her greatest poetry: "Most of her poems grapple at first hand—the more audaciously the better—with the very mysteries of life and death. . . ." [These remarks of Higginson's appear in *The Christian Union*, XLII (September, 1890), 392-93; most critics subsequently referred to are listed in the Bibliography at the end of this volume.] Higginson, in his preface to the volume assembled with Mrs. Todd in 1890, points out that, in the words of Emerson, Emily Dickinson's poetry is "poetry of the portfolio," that written with no design toward publication. He goes on to say that "such verse must inevitably forfeit whatever advantage lies in the discipline of public criticism and the enforced conformity to accepted ways. On the other hand, it may often gain something through the habit of freedom and the unconventional utterance of daring thoughts." His words—that is, his last words, dating after her death and the correspondence with her—on her poetry itself are interesting: "It is believed that the thoughtful reader will find in these pages a quality more suggestive of the poetry of William Blake than of anything to be elsewhere found, —flashes of wholly original and profound insight into nature and life; words and phrases exhibiting an extraordinary vividness of descriptive and imaginative power, yet often set in a seemingly whimsical or even rugged frame. . . . In many cases these verses will seem to the reader like poetry torn up by the roots, with rain and dew and earth still clinging to them, giving a freshness and a fragrance not otherwise to be conveyed. . . . But the main quality of these poems is that of extraordinary grasp and insight, uttered with an uneven vigor sometimes exasperating, seemingly wayward, but really unsought and inevitable. After all, when a thought takes one's breath away, a lesson on grammar seems an impertinence." These values, in effect, are what later critics were to appreciate, too, and also go on to decipher and clarify.

HOWELLS, THOMPSON, LANG. William Dean Howells, for example, a turn-of-the-century critic, appreciated Emily Dickinson's position in the general culture of New England, with a focus on the Puritan spirit. He wrote of her poems that "such things could have come only from a woman's heart to which the experiences in a New England town have brought more knowledge of death than of life. Terribly unsparing many of these strange poems are, but true as the grave and certain as mortality." Of her "rough" or "broken" form he says, "It is the soul of an abrupt, exalted New England woman that speaks in such brokenness." A critic like Maurice Thompson, however, could not overlook these roughnesses; of her now-famous "off-rhymes," for example, he says (the poem is "I taste a liquor never brewed"), "The rhyming of *pearl* with *alcohol* is ludicrous; but the syllable *dure* when set to match *door* cannot be received by any ear that is not hopeless defective." He prefers, of course, identical rhyme, as his era of poets and critics ordinarily did; the modern tendency toward free verse and little rhyme is more able to appreciate Dickinson's off-rhymes. And Andrew Lang, literary man, journalist and anthropologist, displays that spirit of British discipline which colonized and conquered "savagery": "This is certainly a very curious little book. It has already reached its fourth edition, partly, no doubt, because of Mr. Howells, because, if poetry is to exist at all, it really must have form and grammar, and must rhyme when it professes to rhyme. The wisdom of the ages and the nature of man insist on so much. We may be told that Democracy does not care, any more than the Emperor did, for grammar. But even if Democracy overleaps itself and lands in savagery again, I believe that our savage successors will, though unconsciously, make their poems grammatical." It might be added in mild justice that Lang was trained in classical literary scholarship and had a general distrust of the "new realism" exhibited by Howells and other American (and European) writers. To be a classicist is, usually, to be committed to ideas of "order" and traditional order at that. No wonder Lang could find only "nonsense" in Emily Dickinson's queer combinations of words and her off-rhymes; to him she was mostly "fantastic" and "irresponsible."

CRITICISM: 1901-1930.   Conrad Aiken, an accomplished poet himself, was among those critics of the twenties and thirties who began to see the Emily Dickinson "question" as complicated. He was unable to concede, for instance, that her seclusion sprang entirely from a disappointed love affair; and, although as interested as any other reader in biographical incidents, he was dissatisfied with the random anecdotes that come down to us from relatives and friends about her, insisting quite rightly that they do not make up a whole case. He is willing merely to admit that "she was longing for poetic sympathy"; that there were "causes of the psychic injury which so sharply turned her in upon herself," but about them we can only speculate; that "she suffered acutely from intellectual drought . . . perpetually in retreat, always discovering anew, with dismay, the intellectual limitations of her correspondents; that she took "perverse pleasure," given what she saw as an unresponsive society, in her cryptic style. He sees her as a "singular mixture" of Puritan and free thinker," whose most remarkable poems were written on the subject of time, death and immortality: "Death profoundly and cruelly invited her," he remarks, startlingly but truly. And, as is now generally agreed, her genius was "as erratic as it was brilliant."

THE MODERN CRITICS.   Percy Lubbock, whose *The Craft of Fiction* is a masterpiece in the theory of modern fiction (writing in 1924), saw her with judicious sympathy. He observes, "As for her strange little poems, they too suffered in the end from the perverse artificiality of her life. Their cryptic harshness, their bad rhymes and wild grammar—Emily came to believe, perhaps, that these were a mark of her originality and sincerity, disdaining rule. Her friends believed so, at any rate, and she hardly encountered the criticism of any but her friends." He concludes rather nicely on what is the "spirit" of this poet: "To this determined little anchoress, so carefully shut up in her provincial cell, nothing was sacred and nothing daunting; she made as free with heaven and hell, life and death, as with the daisies and butterfles outside her window. She was small, she was obstinate, she was not as wise as she ended by thinking herself; but her voice was unique, and she flung out the short cry of her joy or pain or mockery with a note that cannot be forgotten. It is much to say in a world where voices are so many."

LIKENESS TO METAPHYSICALS. Theodore Spencer (in 1929) likened her to the metaphysical poets of the 17th century, John Donne and George Herbert, who were mystics, rather than to the spirit of her own time; and he praised her epigrammatic quality. George Whicher, who has written extensively about her, observed in her "passion for immediacy" her insistent impulse to make what is abstract concrete and direct.

CONTEMPORY CRITICISM: 1931-PRESENT. A. C. Ward (author of *American Literature: 1880-1930*) places Dickinson within the context of the cultural and literary history of the United States, focussing on her belief in the "inviolability of selfhood." He places her at an opposite pole from a vulgar, hurrying and materialistic America of the end of the 19th century. "She was not, it is clear, a resigned and long-suffering spinster who took the world as she found it. To the world she may have appeared placid and acquiescent, because it was within her Self that the drama was played and judgements passed. . . . Emily Dickinson's real force lay in her almost contemptuously detached manner of stating truths. . . ." Allen Tate, a very influential critic and teacher of our century, also compares her to the 17th century metaphysical poets, and suggests she is primarily a poet of personal revelation—this, rather than moralizing or philosophizing, was her primary move. She can be as impersonal (objective, detached), however, as she can be subjective and personal; and her best work exhibits an "intellectual toughness, a hard, definite sense of the physical world. The highest flights to God, the most extravagant metaphors of the strange and the remote, come back to a point of casuistry, to a moral dilemma of the experienced world. . . . Her poetry is a magnificent personal confession, blasphemous and, in its self-revelation, its honesty, almost obscene. It comes out of an intellectual life towards which it feels no moral responsibility. Cotton Mather would have burnt her for a witch." Interesting commentary, although a bit exhilarated and extreme. Yvor Winters, considered an intriguing, stimulating yet somewhat unorthodox critic, is able to treat very strictly her defects and her virtues. He admits that her technique is often "barbarous" and "irresponsible." (His analysis of her poetry, line for line, is very useful.) Of that "obscurity" which Andrew Lang was so impatient and adversely critical, Winters has some interesting comments. "This unpredictable boldness in plunging into obscurity, a boldness in part, perhaps, inherited from the earlier New Englanders whose sense of divine guidance was so highly developed, whose humility of spirit was commonly so small . . . may have led her to attempt the rendering of purely theoretic experience, the experience of life after death. . . ." The idea of a "small humility," attributable to Puritanism, seems valid, given Emily Dickinson's conflicting desire to be unnoticed and noticed.

OTHER OPINIONS.   Austin Warren's essay-review of Thomas H. Johnson's *The Poems of Emily Dickinson* in 1955 (published in 1957) is to be highly recommended in its coverage of many aspects: relevance of her biography, importance of definitive texts, variety of themes, general poetic significance. For example, Warren makes an interesting point on her "development" (critics usually try to determine if a writer's style has developed, and progressed, over the years of their production). Before the Johnson edition, Warren had "postulated a consistency of method: expected the poems systematically to grow more Dickinsonian. Having achieved her manner, her best style, she could not, I supposed, have turned back to styles not so definitely hers. This theory was too neat. Emily did, to the end, 'look back.' " For us as readers this simply explains the mixture of excellent and average and very poor poems we often find in anthologies. Warren validly concludes, "Emily added to her styles without subtracting; and in maturity she wrote a new kind of poetry without relinquishing the liberty of slipping back

into her earlier modes." On Dickinsonian biographical speculation Warren is similarly illuminating, and ironically witty. He
begins, "I heartily wish that conjecture about Emily's lovers
might cease as unprofitable: of course she wrote out of her life,
her life on various levels. But books on who her 'lover' was turn
attention from the poems to the poet, and substitute detective
work for criticism. Her readers of the 1890's did not require to
know what 'who' or 'whos' gave her insight into love and renunciation, nor need we." Mr. Warren is supplying here a timely
reproach to all who would obscure the literary excellence (or
poverty) of a poem in order to uncover the gossip in the background: the *"is"* rather than the *"why"* of a poem must come
first. Yet Warren proceeds to observe in a pleasingly practical
fashion upon this very speculation. He concludes, though, from
all good evidence which has now been assembled, that the Reverend Wadsworth "certainly mattered to Emily; and the time of
his removal from Philadelphia to San Francisco, a distance pro-
hibitive of prompt access to him by letter, coincides with significant alterations in her life and poetry. Yet this was a fantasy
of love, constructed about a man whom she scarcely knew and
who was doubtless never aware of her idealization." This seems
a sensible conclusion about that oft-discussed "relationship,"
placing the focus where it belongs.

R. P. BLACKMUR.   One of R. P. Blackmur's most piercing
insights into Emily Dickinson (long a professor of English at
Princeton, Blackmur was one of the eminent and most original
critics of our time) is that her poetry is "actualized experience"
—"Imagination, if it works at all, works at the level of actualized
experience." This is akin to what Austin Warren has called her
sense of the "immediacy of experience." Blackmur admits, as
we all must, that she was inconsistent and undisciplined; but, as
he points out, she was neither professional nor amateur, and
her success and failure may be "accidental largely because of
the private and eccentric nature of her relation to the business
of poetry . . . she was a private poet who wrote indefatigably as
some women cook or knit. Her gift for words and the cultural

predicament of her time drove her to poetry. . . . She came at
the right time for one kind of poetry: the poetry of sophisticated,
eccentric vision. That is what makes her good—in a few poems
and many passages representatively great. But she never under-
took the great profession of controlling the means of objective
expression. . . . The pity of it is that the document her whole
work makes shows nothing so much as that she had the themes,
the insight, the observation, and the capacity for honesty, which
had she only known how—or only known why—would have
made the major instead of the minor fraction of her verse genuine poetry. But her dying society had no tradition by which to
teach her the one lesson she did not know by instinct."

DICKINSON AS AMERICAN POET.   Thus we return to the
idea of Emily Dickinson as "paradox," as the representative of
divided and ambiguous things. It is an American trait, if we
consider the split in the American consciousness between idealism (echoes of both Puritan Christianity and American Transcendentalism, along with the "American dream," of pioneer
conquest and cultivation of rewards from the great reaches of
land) and "pragmatism" (the materialistic core of American
life; the other part of that American dream, that every boy can
be president; and, more importantly to a true definition of pragmatism, the clear-eyed capacity to look at life as it really is, not
as it ought to be or we'd wish it to be). That these elements
would be in conflict, in American society generally and in Emily
Dickinson or other American writers particularly, is inevitable.
Not so surprising, then, that she was both Puritan and freethinker, desirous of listeners yet perversely secretive, devoted to
poetry yet rebellious to its rules, brilliantly concise yet indiffer-
ently redundant, sharply ironic yet sillily sentimental, original
and trite.

ESSAY QUESTIONS AND ANSWERS
FOR REVIEW

1. Who was Thomas Wentworth Higginson?

Higginson was an essayist, chiefly for the *Atlantic Monthly* during the period that concerns us here—a rising young man of letters. In 1862, responding to Higginson's interest in young writers expressed in an essay, Emily Dickinson wrote to him enclosing verses and asking him to tell her "if it was alive." There followed an intriguing correspondence, with the burden of it borne mostly by Emily Dickinson, who was pathetically eager for a friend and a mentor, even if she did not intend to take his advice, as some of her replies to his reproaches of "waywardness" in her versifying indicate. These letters are a quaint and somewhat touching document, quite as illustrative of the personality of Dickinson as her poetry is: she signs her name as "Your Scholar" or sometimes "Your Gnome," and she may write at length or just two lines: "Dear Friend,—Mother was paralyzed Tuesday, a year from the evening father died. I thought perhaps you would care. Your Scholar."

Her need for a literary friend, an observer from outside, was great, probably greater than she realized. But Higginson was a busy man, and there is no indication that he completely understood her poetry. He saw her only twice, visiting her in Amherst, an interview about which he later commented in an *Atlantic* essay. After her death he helped put together the first slim volume of her poems to be published, and there again commented —this time more generously—on her poetic worth, saying, "After all, when a thought takes one's breath away, a lesson on grammar seems an impertinence."

2. Emily Dickinson's "love life" has been much speculated upon in the past. What would you say in the general consensus of today's more thoughtful critics on this subject?

97

Disappointing as it may be to some "literary bodysnatchers," it would seem that there is no clear, factual evidence for supposing that Emily Dickinson chose to live a withdrawn life simply on the basis of a love disillusionment. As a young schoolgirl, she had two friends, Leonard Humphrey and Benjamin Newton, who took an interest in her and her writing. These men died young, and it is possible she makes reference to them in some of her poems, such as "My life closed twice before its close." It is fairly well estalished that she met and became infatuated with the Reverend Wadsworth, a married man and a father, in the mid-1850's, evidenced partly by drafts of letters she wrote which survive (although no returning correspondence from Wadsworth remains, if there was any). Her so-called "love poems" certainly indicate an acute mental anguish and intense feelings of deprivation from a love object; but the most judicious assessment of the "relationship" with Wadsworth is that he became idealized in Emily Dickinson's mind—she seems to have remained little-girl-like in her need to idolize and look up to men, especially men slightly older than she. Her love for him, while undoubtedly intense and real to her, was chiefly a fantasy love, just as the loss she suffered by his removal from the East to San Francisco to a ministry (since after all she had had little real contact with the man) was intensified by her own imagination and her seclusion from any other companions. Late in life, after her father's death, she seems to have conceived a similar idealized passion for a Judge Otis P. Lord of Salem; that he was an old and familiar friend of the family, and that it occurred after her father's death (Mr. Dickinson was certainly a dominant figure in her life, as much a "love figure" as any of the above-mentioned men) are surely significant. No union of course resulted from this "relationship," either, although 15 surviving drafts of letters verify its existence.

3. In the past a great deal has been made of Emily Dickinson's sequestered life. Comment on this, in an attempt to sort out fact and mere speculation.

It is true that in her mid-twenties Emily Dickinson began to live a more secluded life, out of society—a letter of this period states, for example, "I go not from home." About her girlhood and schooldays (and she received an exceptional education for a girl of her time), though, the comments of friends and relative which we have been able to gather together indicate that although she was shy, she was also considered lively and witty. It is safe to conclude that since her father was an Amherst lawyer and later Treasurer of Amherst College as well as a member of the state legislature, much of Amherst "society" made its way to the Dickinson home. Emily did grow increasingly withdrawn, though—during her correspondence with Higginson, for example, she makes it clear that if he wishes to meet her, he will have to come to her. It is generally concluded by critics that hers was, for a variety of circumstances, an introverted personality: some of these circumstances may be the very dominant father in the Dickinson household (neither of the daughters ever married); the era itself, which made for more seclusion of young girls than we comprehend today; and the sum of losses which Emily Dickinson felt she had suffered, through death of or separation from friends. There is indication, then, that her life may have been thwarted into seclusion, but not so much more than the lives of other young women of the time. Late in life, however, particularly after the death of her father in 1874, she became a complete recluse and somewhat morbid in her pre-occupation with the theme of death and immortality.

4. Comment on the text and the editing of Emily Dickinson's poetry.

Only a few of her poems were published in her lifetime, although the first slim collection appeared several years after her death, with subsequent volumes following closely in the next few years, mostly assembled—"edited"—by relatives and friends. Fortunately for the preservation and publication of some "authoritative" text of her poems, all manuscripts and letters were acquired by Harvard University in 1950, after which Thomas H. Johnson edited what is generally known as the authoritative or definitive edition of the poems and letters, in three volumes, in 1955. To compare Johnson's texts of the poems with other previous editions is to understand how the words and lines had sometimes been unduly tampered with in the past. Added problems of editing Dickinson's poetry are that most of it appeared in her own handwriting, which altered almost from year to year; and that she was inclined to excessive use of capital letters and to unorthodox punctuation, so that any editor has to decide how much to change and how much to leave as is.

5. What seems to have been Emily Dickinson's attitude toward the Calvinist religion of her day (represented by the "Orthodox Church" of the New England area)?

Her attitude seems to have been ambivalent: she both believed and doubted, for example, from the evidence of her poems and her correspondence. As she once wrote (to Higginson), "That bareheaded life under grass worries one like a wasp." In other words, she had difficulty accepting the rigid beliefs of the Trinitarian Congregationalist Church to which most of her community and some of her family belonged; and her doubts lay especially in the direction of "faith," the nature of death and the afterlife. An example is the semi-serious poem, "Faith is a fine invention/ For gentlemen who see;/ But microscopes are prudent/ In an emergency." It should be pointed out, though, that some of her most powerful poetry was produced out of this kind of schizophrenia she felt about impermanence and immortality. Some examples are "Because I could not stop for Death/ He kindly stopped for me," sometimes called "The Chariot"; "I never saw a moor"; and, in the later more morbid strain, demonstrating her intense curiosity about the nature of death, such poems as "To know just how he suffered would be dear."

The influence of the Calvinist tradition upon her thought is not only seen in the poems about death; ideas such as punishment, renunciation, remorse, and payment for pleasure pervade her work; in fact, examples can be found for all of the above-mentioned ideas: "For each ecstatic instant/ We must an anguish pay"; "Renunciation/ Is a piercing virtue"; "Remorse is memory awake."

6. Comment on the themes of love, loss, pain and despair in Emily Dickinson's poetry.

Certainly the idea of pain and deprivation is the second most obsessive theme, after time, death and immortality, in her poetry. Often a seeming love loss is depicted, and pain and despair are intertwined. For example, "My life closed twice before its close" apparently refers to the early death of two young men friends, Leonard Humphrey and Benjamin Newton;. and "I never lost as much but twice/ And that was in the tomb." Furthermore, there are poems which frankly attempt to describe "pain," which we take to be "mental anguish" to this poet: "Pain has an element of blank," which treats the futile, all-encompassing aspects of pain. "It was not death, for I stood up" is a powerful rendering of her obsessive idea of death in life; here she compares a condition of loss or pain to that of being dead, or de-animated. The poem which seems to refer most directly to her thwarted love for the Reverend Wardsworth is "I cannot live with you," which goes on in sequence to explain "I cannot die with you," "I could not rise with you," concluding in one of her most excellent stanzas anywhere, "So we must keep apart. . . ." Out of all this conviction of suffering emerged a stoicism, too, as evidenced in such a poem as "Superiority to fate/ Is difficult to learn"; but at length the soul, with surprise, "with strict economy/ Subsists till Paradise."

7. Comment on the three following poems, which elude classification under "Nature," "Time, death and immortality," or "Life": "It can't be summer,—that got through"; "There's a certain slant of light"; "As imperceptibly as grief."

The first-mentioned poem seems to be concerned with the advent of fall and winter, "that long town of white to cross/ Before the blackbirds sing." Its second stanza expresses similar doubt about the sunset, which seems too "rouge" for a dying day, since "The dead shall go in white." The whole poem seems to be a metaphor of Emily Dickinson's "death-in-life" concept of living (she "went in white" during her later years, like the Oriental lovers who have been through tribulation and washed their robes white). And "blackbirds" is a suggestion of death.

"There's a certain slant of light" is one of her most exquisite poems, ostensibly about the light of late winter afternoons and the feeling it evokes. But this feeling is oppressive, like "cathedral tunes," and it gives "heavenly hurt," deep in the soul. Later in the poem she says this winter light is "the seal, despair/ An imperial affliction/ sent us of the air," making it fairly clear that she equates the winter light with death. This is proven by the last stanza, which describes the moment of the coming and the going of that light. "When it goes, 'tis like the distance/ On the look of death." It is certainly a nature poem; but it has an exact correspondence with an intuition about time and death.

"As imperceptibly as grief" purports to describe how the summer "lapsed away," but the keynote is time, and imperceptible change in general (first suggested, perhaps, in the word *grief*). The stanzas build a quiet pathos, by "quietness distilled" and "sequestered afternoon," and by morning, personified, as a "guest" who with "a courteous, yet harrowing grace . . . would be gone." Again, the literal meaning is that the days are growing shorter, and dawn comes later; but when the reader at the close of the poem, given summer's "light escape/ Into the beautiful," contemplates the fuller meaning, it emerges as a commentary on the sadly imperceptible passage of human time.

8. Discuss Emily Dickinson's poetic technique.

Emily Dickinson is one of the most difficult poets to discuss in terms of poetic technique, because of the editing which has been done to her poems and because she wrote her poetry on any scrap of paper that was handy. She has an unorthodox, individual style, however, which can be commented on to some extent at least. The basic rhythm of her lines is iambic tetrameter, or eight syllables with four beats per line ("Because/ I could/ not stop/ for Death/"). She is changeable in her punctuation and capitalization; often she uses dashes instead of periods, and she seemed to capitalize words at will. Most of her poems are short, but deceptively so; that is, she comments significantly on some aspect of human life in a brief, succinct statement. She is also very condensed; that is, she often omits many words in a sentence, leaving only the essential words from which the meaning must be deduced.

9. What was Emily Dickinson's idea as to the function of the artist?

Although her poetry was written for publication, Emily Dickinson was very serious in her idea about the duty of the artist. In her own words, the poet must "tell the truth, but tell it slant." In other words, the poet must see reality as it actually is, in all its pain and beauty, and he must put down this truth in his works. He must not make an explicit, or obvious, statement, however; he must tell the truth "slant," by suggestion rather than by statement. A look at her poetry reveals that she practiced this rule consistently. One of her favorite poetic devices is writing an entire poem in definition of an object which is never mentioned; "I like to see it lap the miles," for example, describes a train, yet the word train never appears in the poem. She is rarely overtly critical in her poetry; "Faith is a fine invention" and "Safe in their alabaster chambers" treat religion sardonically, for example, yet they do not bluntly state that faith is foolishness or that religion deadens the feelings. Her idea of the poet, then, was a person who saw and wrote the truth, but always by suggestion rather than by direct statement.

10. In what sense could Emily Dickinson be called a Transcendentalist?

Emily Dickinson's thought has often been compared to Transcendentalism, the 19th century philosophy-religion of nature made famous by Ralph Waldo Emerson and Henry David Thoreau. Transcendentalists believed in a very personal, one-to-one relationship with God, a relationship which could best be nourished by an intimate, long-lasting contact with nature. They believed in an intuitive faith rather than a coldly rational one, a faith of the heart, which can commune with God's creatures, rather than of the head, which must reason from books. The Transcendentalists also held that the truest worship of God took place, not in cold marble churches, but out of doors, where God's works are to be seen and touched.

Emily Dickinson shows many of the characteristics of Transcendentalism, though she was not specifically linked with the movement during her lifetime. Her distrust of organized religion can be seen in "Safe in their alabaster chambers"; her belief that God can be intuited can be found in "I never saw a moor." The poem which begins "Much madness is divinest sense/ To a discerning eye;/ Much sense the starkest madness," is very similar to Emerson's statements of distrust of reason. "Much madness" is the statement of an individual, a person who trusts her own intuition rather than other people's heads, and can be compared with much of Emerson's and Thoreau's poetry.

Her Transcendental idea of poetic inspiration can be seen in "I taste a liquor never brewed." Here she again, like Emerson, praises the intuition, this time as the force which results in good poetry. She speaks of becoming drunk on air and summer days and flowers; this is a direct statement that the poet must become inspired by, in fact drunk on, the natural world.

11. Discuss Emily Dickinson as a Nature poet.

That nature was a constant inspiration to Emily Dickinson is obvious; nearly all of her poetry deals with nature, if not in depth, then at least briefly. She does not merely rhapsodize about nature's beauties, however; she treats it in all aspects and for several different purposes. In "A narrow fellow in the grass," for example, she simply looks at a snake and describes him with wit, close observation, and a brief acknowledgement of the psychological threat that she sees in him. In "I taste a liquor never brewed," she describes the beauties of nature, the joys of a summer's day or an intensely blue sky. But she knows more than one side of nature; in "The sky is low, the clouds are mean," she pictures the world on a dull, menacing day, a day which will end with a snowstorm. Here nature is complaining and unlovely, as well as quite unfriendly to the human observer.

Nature is also used as a stepping-stone to many philosophical observations. For example, "There's a certain slant of light" begins simply with a description of winter light, but very soon becomes a statement on the nature of despair and isolation.

12. Discuss Emily Dickinson's use of the specific detail.

One of Emily Dickinson's greatest talents was her use of the minute, specific detail in order to suggest a general truth. This technique can be seen in so simple a poem as "A narrow fellow in the grass," where she describes a snake (without ever mentioning the word "snake") that anyone might see in a New England meadow, but ends with a chilling generalization; each time she sees the snake, she is reminded of the menacing symbol that he is to the Christian. The same effective use of detail can be seen in "I asked no other thing," where she conveys her sense of deep despair and frustration simply by mentioning that the "mighty merchant" reacts to her request by twirling his button and looking aside. Her own statement on the importance of the individual detail can be seen in "To make a prairie," where she says (with humor, but seriously) that one clover and one bee are all that is necessary to make a prairie.

BIBLIOGRAPHY AND GUIDE TO RESEARCH

Allen, Gay Wilson. "Emily Dickinson's Versification," in *American Prosody*. New York, 1935.

Anderson, Charles R. *Emily Dickinson's Poetry: Stairway of Surprise*. New York, 1960. Representative of modern critics who assume her greatness and go on to discover elements of her poetic method.

Bingham, Millicent Todd. *Ancestors' Brocades: The Literary Debut of Emily Dickinson*. New York, 1945. Lists reviews and criticisms of the 1890's and gives interesting family background.

Blackmur, Richard P. "Emily Dickinson: Notes on Prejudice and Fact," in *Language and Gesture*. New York, 1952. A stimulating, imaginative yet precise critique.

Blake, Caesar R. and Carlton F. Wells. *The Recognition of Emily Dickinson*. Ann Arbor, Mich., 1964. A useful collection of essays on the poet, dating from 1890 to the present.

Dickinson, Emily. *The Poems of Emily Dickinson,* ed. Thomas H. Johnson. 3 vols. Cambridge, Mass., 1955. The authoritative edition.

————. *Selected Poems of Emily Dickinson,* Intro. by Conrad Aiken. New York. A Modern Library book. Aiken's essay is useful criticism, but the arrangement by numbering the poems is difficult to handle.

————. *Selected Poems and Letters by Emily Dickinson,* ed. Robert N. Linscott. New York, 1959. A useful paperback, with indexing by first lines at the end of the book.

Hicks, Granville. "Emily Dickinson and the Gilded Age," in *The Great Tradition*. New York, 1933. Criticism by a Marxist critic whose views have since been modified toward broader principles.

Higginson, Thomas Wentworth. "An Open Portfolio," *The Christian Union*, XLII (September 25, 1890), 392-93.

————. "Preface" to *Poems by Emily Dickinson*. New York, 1890. In collaboration with Mabel Loomis Todd.

Howells, William Dean. "The Strange Poems of Emily Dickinson," *Harper's New Monthly Magazine*. LXXXII (January, 1891), 318-20. A near-contemporary evaluation, showing high regard for her poetry, by a critic and novelist of eminent stature.

Lubbock, Percy. "Determined Little Anchoress," *Nation and Athenaeum*. XXXVI (October 18, 1924), 114. An evaluation of the twenties, calling her brilliantly unique, and indicating the progress of her reputation from that of an eccentric in the 1890's.

Macleish, Archibald. "The Private World," *Emily Dickinson: Three Views*. Amherst, 1960. With Louise Bogan and Richard Wilbur. An anniversary volume.

Matthiessen, F. O. "The Private Poet: Emily Dickinson," *Kenyon Review,* II (Autumn, 1945), 584-97. A careful and imaginative essay by a very reliable critic.

Spencer, Theodore. "Concentration and Intensity," *New England Quarterly*. II (July, 1929), 498-501. Concerned with the texts of the poems.

Tate, Allen. "New England Culture and Emily Dickinson," *Symposium,* III (April, 1932), 206-26. Discusses her as representative of an American cultural tradition.

Thompson, Maurice. "Miss Dickinson's Poems," *America,* V (January, 1891), 425. A view of the period, that she was accidentally successful in spite of unorthodoxies.

Todd, Mabel Loomis. Preface to *Poems: Second Series.* New York, 1891. The first editor who worked patiently toward the initial volume, with Thomas Wentworth Higginson.

Ward, A. C. "A Major American Poet," in *American Literature: 1880-1930.* London, 1932. Connects the greatness of her poetry with the cultural and literary history of her period and beyond in America. A useful essay.

Warren, Austin. "Emily Dickinson," *Sewanee Review,* LXV (Autumn, 1957), 565-86. This essay-review of Johnson's edition summarizes major trends in Dickinsonian criticism, and is well-written

Whicher, George F. "A Centennial Appraisal," in *Emily Dickinson: A Bibliography.* Amherst, 1930. A summary essay for the period, by an expert on the poet.

――――. "Emily Dickinson Among the Victorians," in *Poetry and Civilization.* Ithaca, N.Y., 1955. Toward a historical perspective.

――――. *This Was a Poet.* New York, 1938. One of the earliest and best critical/biographical studies.

Winters, Yvor. "Emily Dickinson and the Limits of Judgment," in *Maule's Curse.* Norfolk, Conn., 1938. Useful in honest treatment of virtues and defects.

NOTES

NOTES

MONARCH®
NOTES AND STUDY GUIDES

ARE AVAILABLE AT RETAIL
STORES EVERYWHERE

In the event your local bookseller
cannot provide you with other
Monarch titles you want —

ORDER ON THE FORM BELOW:

Complete order form appears
on inside front & back covers
for your convenience.

Simply send retail price, local
sales tax, if any, plus 35¢ per
book to cover mailing and
handling.

TITLE #	AUTHOR & TITLE (exactly as shown on title listing)	PRICE
	PLUS ADDITIONAL 35¢ PER BOOK FOR POSTAGE	
	GRAND TOTAL	$

MONARCH® PRESS, a Simon & Schuster Division of Gulf & Western Corporation
Mail Service Department, 1230 Avenue of the Americas, New York, N.Y.   10020

I en .... to cover retail price, local sales tax, plus mailing
and h......

Name _____
(Please print)

Address _____

City _____ State _____ Zip _____

Please send check or money order. We cannot be responsible for cash.